TED DEKKER

THE WAY OF LOVE

RE-DISCOVERING
THE ONLY PATH
TO PEACE IN THIS LIFE

BOOK TWO

Copyright © 2018 by Ted Dekker

Published by Outlaw Studios

All rights reserved. No part of this book may be reproduced in any manner whatsoever without written permission, except in the case of brief quotations embodied in critical articles and reviews.

Unless otherwise indicated, all Scripture quotations are from the New American Standard Bible®, Copyright © 1960, 1962, 1963, 1968, 1971, 1972, 1973, 1975, 1977, 1995 by The Lockman Foundation. Used by permission. (www.Lockman.org)

Scripture quotations marked (NIV) are taken from the Holy Bible, New International Version®, NIV®. Copyright © 1973, 1978, 1984, 2011 by Biblica, Inc.™ Used by permission of Zondervan. All rights reserved worldwide. www.zondervan.com The "NIV" and "New International Version" are trademarks registered in the United States Patent and Trademark Office by Biblica, Inc.™

Scripture quotations marked (ESV) are from the Holy Bible, English Standard Version® (ESV®), copyright © 2001 by Crossway, a publishing ministry of Good News Publishers. Used by permission. All rights reserved.

Scripture quotations marked (KJV) are taken from the Holy Bible, King James Version. Public Domain.

Printed in the U.S.A.

ISBN 978-0-9968124-5-0

CONTENTS

Our Practice	5
Introduction	7

SECTION ONE

The Essentials	11
The Five Seals of Truth	37

SECTION TWO

The Story of Reality in Thirty-six Words	41

THE DEVOTIONAL

Practicing the Forgotten Way	59
1. I Conform to Love	61
2. The Love That Heals Us All	65
3. I Release The Masks I Wear	69
4. The Useless Law I No Longer Follow	73
5. I Am In The Name of Christ	77
6. I Come Like a Little Child	83
7. I Am Grateful For My Struggles	87
8. I Leave the Old Behind	91
9. My New Operating System	95
10. I Have Ears to Hear	99

11. I Lift My Eyes And See A New World	105
12. I Am In Perfect Peace	109
13. My Old Self Is Dead	113
14. I Embrace The Mystery	117
15. The Tigers That Stalk Me	121
16. The Thief Will Not Steal My Love And Grace	125
17. Innocent by Reason of Insanity	129
18. My Resistance is Futile	133
19. As I Align, I Am Being Saved	137
20. My Daily Feast	141
21. I Welcome the Coming of The Son	145
22. I Offer Christ's Love to All	151
23. I Call No Man on Earth Father	155
24. All is Made New	161
The Journey Forward	165
From Darkness to Light	171
The Five Seals of Truth	175
Endnotes	177

OUR PRACTICE

*A time will come when men will not tolerate sound doctrine,
but with itching ears they will gather around themselves
teachers to <u>suit their own desires</u>.*
(Because the human heart is addicted to the law and returns to it
like a dog returns to its vomit. But now we return to love.)
2 Timothy 4:3, BSB

*Love is the fulfillment of the law . . . it is already the hour
for you to <u>awaken</u> from sleep; for now salvation is nearer
to us than when we first believed.* Romans 13:10–11

*God is <u>light</u> and in Him there is no darkness at all. If we say we
have fellowship with Him and yet walk in darkness, we lie and
do not <u>practice</u> the truth.* 1 John 1:5–6

But the one <u>practicing</u> the truth comes to the Light.
Yeshua, John 3:21, BLB

This is our Practice: *to see and awaken to the light
and so love as He loves.*
This is our Journey: *to walk in the light of love
rather than walk in darkness.*

INTRODUCTION

The Way of Love is a journey of re-discovering the only path to peace in this life, as prescribed so clearly by Jesus yet mostly forgotten by we who say we follow in His way. The journey spans two books: *The Way of Love Book One*, and *The Way of Love Book Two*. If you're reading this, you've already sat with Book One at least once. If you haven't, please read Book One first. This second book builds on the first.

Some may wonder why we've broken *The Way of Love* into two books. A special edition was initially published for readers of *The Forgotten Way* and that edition contained all 45 meditations. But 45 meditations are a lot of material for one book and best encountered in two legs of one journey, each roughly 175 pages.

Book Two in *The Way of Love* is laid out in three sections.

ONE: We begin by rehearsing the primary problem we all face as Christians and explain why following Yeshua (Jesus' original name in Hebrew) is the only way to find peace and love in this life. We call this section Essentials, repeated from the first book. Even if you've read this section, I suggest you do so again. You will be surprised by how fresh it reads now, having finished Book One. In fact, if you're like me, you might be best served reading it once a month. How easily we forget!

TWO: The second section contains a new perspective on some of the most common words we use within Christendom (such as: fear, love, kingdom of heaven, grace, transformation), many of which have become confusing. We call this section The Story of Reality in Thirty-six Words, also taken from Book One.

If you feel you have a good handle on how we are defining these words, feel free to skim or skip this section as you wish.

THREE: The third and primary section of this book contains 24 new daily meditations that lead us into an experience of the love that Yeshua said would characterize all those in His way. If you have *The Way of Love Journal,* use it as instructed to reflect on your journey out of darkness into light. Although journaling is not required for this journey, you will find significant benefit from doing so as instructed at the end of each meditation. You can find *The Way of Love Journal* at **www.thewayoflove.net.**

All scriptures noted in sections one and two are found in the endnotes.

Along with me, you seek peace and love in this life, and with me you know that they can only be found as we are reborn into a whole new way of life in Christ, a way so easily forgotten each day. So, then, together we resolve to experience our true identities as the sons and daughters of the Father.

In that resolve, we offer love and show grace to all, because only through the love of Christ will we ourselves awaken to who we are in the light. As Paul wrote, *The fulfillment of the law is love. It is already the hour for you to awaken from sleep for now salvation is nearer than when we first believed.*[1]

A new day dawns for us. The light is bright and flows with love.

SECTION ONE

THE ESSENTIALS

We call our journey into love the Forgotten Way because the radical love that empowers us in this life is so easily *forgotten*. We use the term "way" because Jesus' followers called themselves the people of the *Way* in the years after His resurrection before others later began to call them Christians.

If you haven't read my novels *The 49th Mystic* and *Rise of the Mystics*, it's perfectly fine, but know that they show our journey in a way that only story can. Even if you don't normally read novels, I recommend these two as a way to connect deeply with all that is written in this book.

Having said that, they aren't required for your engagement with these pages.

Like Paul the apostle, we all find ourselves the chief of sinners, prone to struggle because life happens in cycles of ease and challenge, highs and lows, remembering and forgetting, often in the space of a single day or hour. Our journey is to awaken from the darkness of those cycles and live in the love of Christ in this life.

This is the journey of transformation, of awakening, of the renewing of our mind. It's a path of discovery, experienced by each of us, together and alone. It is our conversion from victims in a world darkened by deception to overcomers through an awakening to our true identity. As such, the Forgotten Way isn't a set of facts or labels or dogma, but a living, breathing journey on which all Christians find themselves.

The journey from fear to love.

The journey from blindness to sight.

The journey from darkness to light.

On that journey we will find peace in the storms; we will walk on the troubled seas of our lives; we will not be poisoned by the lies of snakes; we will move mountains that appear insurmountable; we will heal all manner of sickness that twists minds and bodies.

Love will flow from us as living waters, because the manifestation of the kingdom of heaven on Earth *is* love. In the end, the journey is to let go of who we *think* we are, to see and so be who we *truly* are right now, in this moment.

Our journey consists of a series of meditations that draw us into an encounter with love, because the mystery of the Kingdom is experienced more than explained. But before we begin, it's important to set the stage.

THE ELEPHANT IN THE ROOM

If there is one elephant in the room among we who call ourselves Christian, it is that what we *think* and *say* we believe often aren't true in the expression of our lives, perhaps most of the time. Ironically, we ourselves are often the last to see this discrepancy. The disparity not only creates conflict deep within us, but it also confuses the world as to what it means to follow Jesus.

We think and say we believe in Jesus, but we are anxious for tomorrow, just like the rest of the world. We think and say we love our neighbor and our enemy, but we are afraid of all that rises against us as much as anyone else.

But, as the apostle John wrote, *there is no fear in love.*[2]

What is fear? Fear is the ruler of this world. It's the fabric of all negativity, the shadow we run from, the wisdom of the world that puts us to bed at night with a hundred cautionary tales. Indeed, fear has become the barometer of our lives, warning us to avoid whatever might cause it to bear its sharp fangs. We know it's there, under our skin, because when something goes wrong, it snarls and we curse it.

In love, there is none of that. In love, we are free from fear in all of its clever disguises.

If we live in fear—and we do most of the time, even unaware—perhaps we don't know love the way we think we do. Perhaps we are still lost to love, and so we are like those whom we accuse of being lost to Christ.

If we don't know love, are we also lost to Christ, who is love?

Yeshua made it plain: the evidence that we are in His way is love. So, then, our experience and expression of love are not only important but also paramount, yes?

But what, exactly, is this critical thing Yeshua called love? One of the primary challenges we have as Christians is the confusion surrounding this word. If we are even remotely interested in experiencing eternal life, understanding Yeshua's teaching on love is critical.

In Scripture, there are three primary kinds of love: *eros*, which is a conditional, erotic love; *phileo*, which is also conditional and represents a deep personal affection for others, such as the love between friends or between husband and wife; and *agape*, which was most often reserved to describe an unconditional, divine love. In this book, we will use *agape* to mean unconditional love.

All are translated simply as love in English, and this creates confusion.

Everyone experiences *phileo* love—the deep affection for a person based on conditions such as their appearance, their personality, their affection for us, their loyalty to us, and on it goes. But this love is based on law, meaning that if the conditions change, our "love" changes with it. For example, we love our spouse *unless* they betray us, at which time we justify our anger against them. We love our bodies *unless* they get sick or ugly. We love our neighbors *unless* they bomb us. *Phileo* is a conditional love with fear of loss baked in. Whether one is Muslim, Christian, or atheistic, all experience this conditional love.

Phileo love is universal and requires no transformation or rebirth.

Agape love, as presented in this book, is a divine love that can only be experienced as we awaken to who we are in Christ. This is the evidence that Yeshua said would be known by those who are reborn into what He called the kingdom of heaven.

Our challenge is that until we experience unconditional love, we are bound by conditional love and we naturally attribute this same kind of love to God. "God will accept me if I do such and such. He will reject me if I slip up." In attributing conditional love to God, we have secretly become afraid of our Father. This keeps us deeply fractured, because it's impossible for us to love what we fear. As stated earlier, there is no fear in love, yes?

We must begin by realizing that unconditional love is the love of God and can be known by us as we awaken to our identity in Him.

When Paul wrote that unless we have love, everything else about our faith means nothing, he used the word *agape* for love—divine love.

Read: *If I . . . understand all mysteries and all knowledge* (all the correct doctrine and beliefs about God and Jesus), *and if I have all faith, so as to remove mountains, but have not love* (agape) *I am nothing. If I give away all I have, and if I deliver up my body to be burned* (loyalty to creed and confession), *but have not love* (agape), *I gain nothing.*[3]

Then Paul defined *agape* using a string of attributes, such as patience and kindness, that culminates in the following staggering pronouncement: (Agape) *is not provoked;* (agape) *takes no account of evil.* (Other translations: *holds no record of wrong.*)[4]

In other words, the love Paul refers to is unconditional, and unless we are experiencing and expressing this divine love, which is totally unnatural to ordinary human experience, everything about our confession and knowledge of faith is worthless. It's a stunning statement that we have forgotten for far too long. Whenever we use the word "love" or "true love" in this book, we refer to this truest kind of love.

When Paul wrote that love takes no account of evil, the Greek word he used for "takes no account of" or "holds no record of" is a legal term that means "doesn't consider evidence for or doesn't take into account." Some say Paul meant that love doesn't hold onto a wrong for very long, or that love doesn't keep score of wrongs, but that misses the point entirely. How long is not very long? One minute? One month? One year? Truly, if we record wrong for even one millisecond, then for that millisecond we are not in true love but in condemnation and fear.

Is this not also true for God? Does He not love us the way He asks us to love others?

Yeshua described true love as showing kindness and grace to others while they are standing against us. It's different from the love we offer those who return our love, which He called the sinner's love.

If you love those who love you, what credit is that to you? For even sinners love those who love them . . . But love your enemies . . . and you will be sons of the Most High (who is love).[5] If, on the other hand, we get angry with another, we are as subject to judgment as a murderer, He taught, because in anger we are as guilty as any murderer.[6]

Staggering. But utterly liberating.

Imagine being in a late-night argument with someone close who has disappointed or hurt you in any way. Before we defend ourselves or point fingers, should we not ask if we are acting in true love ourselves? Perhaps our defense or attack makes us as guilty as the one who has hurt us. So, then, let us all be silent and reconsider our own state of being, lest we perpetuate a kind of madness that keeps us all bound to fear rather than to love.

Do we not all long to experience this love that is able to offer grace and kindness rather than anger even to those who stand against us? It would and will soon change the world, even as we awaken to it and show others the way by being that love.

Yeshua, like Paul, made it clear that this love is the evidence of those who are in His way. *A new commandment I give you: Love* (agape) *one another. As I have loved you, so also must you love one another. By this all men will know that you are My disciples, if you love one another.*[7]

THE VERDICT

If what we have been taught has not led us and Christianity at large to *agape* love, then perhaps it's time to ask why. We must finally understand one thing with absolute certainty: if we show the evidence of informed doctrine and knowledge and confessions of faith, and if we call Him Lord, but don't walk in a love that holds no record of wrong, then we have surely missed the mark and put our faith in something other than God.

Or, as John put it, *if we say we have fellowship with God but walk in darkness, we lie and do not practice the truth.*[8] And walking in darkness can be summed up as failing to follow His commandment to love one another without holding a record of wrong.

Some say they know they are following Yeshua by the knowledge they have learned, announced, and committed their lives to, but this is only a new form of Gnosticism, which claims that special knowledge is the way to God. True love, not special knowledge, is the evidence of those who follow Yeshua.

So we must ask ourselves this one question above all other questions: have we awakened to our Father's love, which shows us and the world that we are being reborn, or are we still lost in the common love that the world knows while we argue doctrine and heresies and point fingers at sinners?

Is such a love even possible? We say, yes, of course! It's the primary evidence of following Yeshua. But to be sure, in our fallen nature, true love is impossible. It can only be known and expressed as we are reborn in and aligned to Christ.

Seeing that our way of life, despite being called Christian, hasn't drawn us into the experience of His love, we humble ourselves and seek the way of Yeshua without condemning ourselves or others, because this is the beginning love.

Imagine that you are standing in a room that represents your entire life. In that room and on the shelves you see all your treasured vases and furniture and trinkets, which represent all that you value or fear, including your own self-image and all of your relationships.

Shadows come and go, dimming the beauty of your treasures, and when a vase falls and breaks, you rush to fix it or bemoan its loss. All your life you try to maintain the well-being of all your treasure because it defines you. Here, love is conditional—if the vase breaks, you have a grievance, yes?

This is the room that holds fear, condemnation, and darkness. Your state of being goes up and down like a yo-yo as you share love with those who return your love, as you defend yourself from those who judge you, as you try your best to sweep the shadows and darkness from that room.

But there's a door to your right and you've been told that this door leads to another room full of the light of true love, which is not provoked and holds no record of wrong. Part of you wants to enter that new room, but the only way to do so is to leave the room that holds all your treasures. This frightens you because you think you might lose everything that you've been taught will keep you safe and make you happy.

You may say the sinner's prayer and stick one foot in that room or cross the threshold. You may well rejoice at your newfound discovery. But then you rush back into your old familiar room. It has all your treasures, you see. You've been trained to protect them and draw comfort from them.

The problem is, you can't be in both rooms at the same time, in the same way that darkness cannot be in light, in the same way that fear cannot be in love. *You cannot serve two masters* at the same time, as Yeshua taught.

Which room do you find yourself in today? The room of conditional love characterized by a fear of loss and darkness, or the room filled with the light of true love, in which there is no fear or record of wrong?

If we say we are reborn and in the room of light but find ourselves judging our spouse when he or she betrays us, holding grievances against those who threaten our idea of safety, cringing when the storms of life rise to crush us, then perhaps we are only lying to ourselves about which room we occupy.

Do you see the problem we face? *We* are the elephant in the room, and the whole world can see which room we inhabit. Is it not finally time to enter the light, which is characterized by, above all things, Christ's love?

In reality, both rooms are in the same place, as we will see, like two dimensions that coexist. The eyes with which we perceive determine which dimension we see.

Yeshua called the dimension of light *the kingdom of heaven.*

A SIMPLE SUMMARY OF THE WORLD WE LIVE IN

Yeshua described reality as consisting of two kingdoms that coexist everywhere at once. They aren't separated by distance, but by perception. We will call one "high" and one "low," as in things above and things below. He called the high one *the kingdom of heaven* or *the light*, and the low one simply *the world*. If you have new eyes to see, you can see the kingdom of heaven. If you don't have eyes to see, you will only see the world you know, the low kingdom.

Read His teaching: *Except anyone be born from above* (some translations: born again), *he is not able to **see** the kingdom of God.*[9] And then a few verses later: *But the one practicing the truth comes to the light.*[10] Entering the "kingdom" and seeing the light is Yeshua's primary way of speaking of our regenerative process from blindness to sight through our *practicing of the truth*.

In other words, we experience the kingdom of heaven, which is the light, as we follow His teachings. Otherwise, we remain in darkness, unable to see that kingdom.

Some think that the kingdom of heaven is yet to come, but consider Yeshua's teaching on the matter: *Now having been questioned by the Pharisees as to when the kingdom of God was coming, He answered them and said,* "**The kingdom of God is not coming with signs** *to be observed; nor will they say, 'Look, here it is!' or, 'There it is!'"*[11]

The kingdom has nothing to do with *where* or *when*. Why? He tells us immediately in His next statement: *"For behold,* **the kingdom of God is within you***."*[12] The word He used for *within* literally means *inside of your very being* or *in the very midst of your being/body*.

Do you follow? This is the kingdom of the light of heaven that can be seen with the eyes of Christ. It's characterized by, above all, a love that holds no record of wrong.

In his letters, the apostle John, like Yeshua, called the kingdom of heaven *the light,* and he called the world *darkness* due to blindness. Read: *The one who loves his brother abides in* **the light** *and there is no cause for stumbling in him. But the one who hates his brother is in the darkness and walks in the darkness, and does not know where he is going* **because the darkness has blinded his eyes***.*[13]

The low kingdom of darkness (the world) is bound by the knowledge of good and evil (the fruit of the fall), which causes judgment, grievance, and fear. In this perception, we are blinded to the light. In that blindness to the kingdom of heaven, we know only conditional love. We might call this "being lost" or "living in sin." It's our natural state of being in this world.

The higher kingdom of heaven is the awareness and experience of the light, the divine in all of its expressions, free from the knowledge of good and evil (the curse of the fall). As we awaken into it—as our minds are transformed to perceive it—we walk in light and true love.

Here, there is no compulsion to condemn or hold others in darkness. Here, we know the love that holds no record of wrong—that supernatural love that is the evidence of being in the light. Yeshua's invitation to us is to see and abide in this kingdom of love and light, beyond what the natural mind can conceive. He called this process "being born from above" or "being born again," depending on the translation.

Again, as Yeshua taught: *Unless a man is born from above* (born again)*, he cannot **see** the kingdom of heaven . . . But the one practicing the truth comes to the light.* Being born again happens as we practice the truth.

It follows, then, that if we aren't *seeing* the light and experiencing a love that holds no record of wrong, we are still quite blind and haven't yet fully awakened to Christ or entered the kingdom of heaven in this life. We continue to stumble in darkness.

As an analogy, think of the caterpillar who crawls on the ground, unknowing that it will enter a womb of sorts (a cocoon) and be reborn as a butterfly. Think of the ground on which the caterpillar crawls as being the system of the world, bound in fear and judgment—the providence of the lower nature.

Think of the air in which the butterfly will take flight as the kingdom of heaven, streaming with love. The caterpillar's perspective of the world and what the butterfly sees are entirely different realities. Both coexist in this life.

Unless the caterpillar enters the cocoon and is reborn as a butterfly, it cannot see the kingdom of heaven now at hand.

Many think that being born again is an instantaneous, one-time event, and while this may be true on one level, it may serve us to think of our *coming into the light* as a process as we practice the truth, like Yeshua taught.

When we first hear the good news and accept it, we are filled with joy, and we call this a conversion experience. And there are many such experiences as we take our journey, so we are glad for that first one, but this is only the beginning of what Yeshua referred to in His analogy of being born again, yes?

The caterpillar doesn't immediately become a butterfly just because it has heard that flying is possible and has agreed to the adventure.

Process is how Yeshua described coming into the experience of the kingdom in His parable of the seeds. In His story, many hear the news and receive it with great joy because it's very real for them. This is like hearing the good news and becoming a Christian, yes? But, as His parable states, later that seedling is often stolen because it hasn't matured. The process is cut short. Blindness returns. Fear overtakes love once more. And so we stumble in darkness, sons and daughters though we are.

The good news for us is that if we think we are born again and stumble in darkness, there is still great transformation available to us! We can still fly. Living as a butterfly is our inheritance. It's our true nature. It's time to stop crawling on the ground so that we can see the kingdom of heaven evidenced by a love in which there is no fear and that holds no record of wrong.

We can surely agree on one thing: any interpretation of Scripture that doesn't lead us to true love leads us to something other than Christ. If we say we have faith in Christ, but the workings of our life don't reflect the love of Christ, perhaps we have put our faith in something other than the light of Christ, at least for the time that we have set aside that love.

So many today say there is too much talk of love coming into Christianity and that we love ourselves too much. But we know in our hearts we are just barely beginning to fathom true love. Our greatest challenge isn't too much self-love, but an abundance of self-loathing. Thus, we have shown all manner of evidence but the true evidence, which is a kind of love we know so little about.

We may have unwittingly cultivated a faith built upon fear rather than love. Judgment and condemnation have become our self-righteousness, and defending our interpretation of Scripture has become a badge of honor. Needing to prove ourselves right has trumped grace, even though we agree that being right means nothing if we aren't expressing true love. Still we insist, driven by fear that we might be wrong. In that fear, we are blinded further to love because, like oil and water, fear and love don't mix. There is no fear in love.

Rather than point fingers at others, let us confess our own fears and embark on a journey that brings us back into the love that holds no record of wrong. Only in that love can we experience the kingdom of heaven while we walk this world as the Father's children.

THE WORD OF GOD

Most of us believe the Word of God without question, and that Word is Christ, through and in whom all that was made exists.[14] When we say the Word is living, active, sharper than any two-edged sword, piercing soul and spirit, we are talking about Christ, who alone is the Word.[15]

We also believe in the inspired written words that we call the Bible, but our interpretation of those words varies dramatically. No one can insist that their interpretation is correct in all respects—that would be the vanity of the intellect asserting itself as a god to be honored. So we humble ourselves and enter into discourse while submitting to the leading of the Spirit, not the authority of any man or institution.

We also know that God is best revealed to little children rather than to the wise and intelligent,[16] so His way must be simple. And we know that, as Jesus said, His yoke (which in His day meant *interpretation of the Scriptures*) is easy and His burden light.[17]

Even as a child intuitively knows a good story and good news, we, too, look for the good news of the Father in a simple story. We become like that small child so that we may know our Father.

The Holy Spirit speaks to us through the Bible, but much of what we glean from its pages is only what we have been taught based on another's interpretation. When someone says, "We only need the Bible," what they most often mean is, "All we need is *my interpretation* of the Bible." When someone says, "Such and such is not biblical and so is heretical," what they're often saying is, "Such and such does match *my interpretation* of what the Bible says, so I will call it heresy."

Are we to trust another person's interpretation because we don't trust ourselves to hear the Word, who is Christ, speaking to us? Are we to put our trust in the interpretations of scholars, or in denominational creeds, or in what our parents have been taught, or in what a group of men decided a thousand years ago? No, because in doing so, we would be putting our faith in man, not in the Spirit of Truth, who is God.[18]

And yet we fear the scorn of man still.

Why do we live in such fear? Perhaps in large part because within a couple hundred years of Yeshua's death, Christianity at large returned to a form of law that demanded man meet certain legal requirements, which were codified and enforced through the pervasive use of torture and widespread persecution of Christians who didn't agree with institutionalized doctrine. Even to ask the wrong question of those enforcers of "truth" was to risk being labeled a heretic and inviting terrible suffering or death.

The gospel that once spread through the power of the Holy Spirit and love became creeds and dogmas that demanded allegiance enforced through fear and control. That fear and control only expanded throughout the next thousand years and still rages today.

But a new day dawns among us all, and the gospel of Christ is being found in love once more. And there is no fear in love. We each work out our salvation through awe, and as we do, we tremble at the wonder of it all.

THE BIBLE

All of this begs the question, what *is* our interpretation of the sacred, inspired collection of writings we call the Bible? So many throw around words like "heresy" and "false doctrine" with little consideration for how doing so manipulates through fear rather than invites through love.

Consider one of our most beloved brothers, the late Billy Graham, who introduced countless millions to the good news. In an interview conducted in 1997, Billy Graham made the following statement regarding salvation, which he still holds to: "I think everybody that loves Christ, or knows Christ, whether they're conscious of it or not, they're members of the Body of Christ . . . They may not even know the name of Jesus but they know in their hearts that they need something that they don't have, and they turn to the only light that they have, and I think that they are saved, and that they're going to be with us in heaven."

Many have since publicly declared Billy Graham a heretic because his beliefs regarding salvation don't line up with their interpretation of what they think the Bible teaches.

Are we to call our Southern Baptist brother a heretic because his interpretation of the Bible differed from our own? Does our Father now stand in condemnation of His son, Billy, who clearly loved the gospel of Yeshua? Dare we suggest that Billy now suffers for what we think was a false belief?

Seeing such a disparity of interpretations of the written Word, how are we to interpret the holy Scriptures?

When Genesis tells us that God walked with Adam and Eve in the garden, did He literally have two legs to walk in a literal garden, or is the Creation story a parable of origin and separation?

Is the Spirit of God actually a great spinning wheel in the heavens as Ezekiel saw Him (see Ezekiel 1:16), or was this metaphorical? Do angels still ride in chariots as seen by the prophet Elisha (see 2 Kings 6:17)? Did they ever actually do so, or was this vision simply presented in imagery that Elisha could understand so long ago?

Is the book of Revelation a prophetic declaration of literal events still to come, as some theologians say, or is it a grand metaphorical analogy describing something that happens in each of our lives, as other scholars claim? Or is it both?

Did the great apostasy that Paul wrote about to the Thessalonians happen when Christianity returned to the systems of fear and law in the fourth and fifth centuries, or is that great turning away something yet to come? Or is it both?

Is the second coming of Christ a radical coming of Christ's revelation and manifestation in the hearts of all over a brief time, or is it going to be a physical, one-time event where Jesus actually floats down from the sky? Or is it both?

Does Yeshua still have a body like ours today, or is it glorified so totally unlike ours, or does He only show Himself to some as a body like God revealed Himself as a wheel within a wheel to Ezekiel? Or is it all of these?

Who experiences hell, and is it a literal place or an experience beyond space and time, thus eternal? Or is it the experience of separation from God in this life? Or is it all of these?

How are we to answer all of these questions? Yes. Perhaps. Maybe not. Of course. Of course not. I'm not sure.

These questions are not the ones we fight over or die for in this book. Dogmatism has spawned enough fear and grievance, and fear itself denies the very Christ that it seeks to defend. The interpretations of scholars according to the traditions of man's intelligence have no end.

I too have a degree in theology, but that doesn't make my interpretations any more valid than those who do not. Our lives, not our arguments, are the evidence of love, and love is the evidence of all who have awakened to Christ.

Let us humble ourselves and realize that in many ways, intellectually speaking, we are like ants on the side of a computer, arguing over how the processor works—the processor being God. So it's rather silly to call the other ants foolish because we too are surely as foolish in many ways. Rather, we stand in awe of the glory of our Father and know Him in love. And we stand in awe of His creation and know all we encounter in that same love.

How then are we to interpret Scripture? First and foremost through the lens of true love, because, once again, any interpretation of Scripture that doesn't lead us to love is likely leading us to something other than Christ. And we do so in humility, each of us willing to be led by the Holy Spirit rather than by our own reasoning based upon what we were taught.

We, like Paul, long to know Christ and the staggering power of His resurrection[19]—and as those who have risen with Him,[20] to know the power of our own resurrection in Him, not as a doctrinal statement or interpretation that satisfies the intellect, but as a reality that empowers us to love as Christ loves.

THE WORDS WE USE

As a boy who grew up as the son of missionaries on an island that had over seven hundred distinct languages, I was surrounded by linguists intent on translating Scripture into each native tongue. In such a setting, the radically subjective nature of all human language becomes blatantly apparent.

To this day, when the Christians where I grew up pray, they begin with, "Aye, Allah Nogobah," which literally means, "Oh, God our Father." They were never Muslim and when they pray, they pray to the same infinite Father we do.

So we may wonder, is their use of the word *Allah,* which means "God" in their language, heretical?

If we are tempted to think so, we must remember that neither Yeshua nor Paul used any of the English words we use to describe God. Yeshua spoke in Aramaic, and His words were written down in Greek. There are no documents that record His actual words in the language He spoke them. We have only the Greek writings, which have subsequently been translated into English along with thousands of other languages. Any English translation is already two languages removed from the actual words Yeshua used.

In fact, Jesus was never called "Jesus" and Paul was never called "Paul." These are English equivalents. None of the early Christians ever once prayed using the name "Jesus." It didn't exist in that part of the world at that time. His Hebrew name was *Yeshua*, and in Greek, *Iesous.*

In this book, we will use the name *Yeshua,* not because it has any particular value over the name "Jesus," but because we choose to use His original name.

However important they are, words are simply symbols that represent an idea behind that symbol. We must remember this. It is the meaning a person associates with a word that matters. It is important that we don't hold our specific words sacred. To hold them sacred is to worship them. We hold Christ as sacred, not the words and symbols that point to Him. This would be idolatry.

In the same way, we don't dismiss an idea just because it's described using words we aren't as familiar with. In fact, new language often helps us reconsider historically entrenched ideas that have lost their power through overuse.

Case in point: the word "enlightenment" to describe a spiritual awakening is used by both Paul the apostle and by many in the New Age movement. The New Age movement makes little sense to me for a number of reasons, but that doesn't mean I throw away all its terms.

Just because we may not agree with another's use of a particular word doesn't mean we are afraid to use it ourselves. Such fear has crippled us for far too long and we now surrender that fear to love.

Should we throw away the word "love" because Hindus use it? Love and grace are at the heart of Christianity. Should we not use the word "energy" because it is used by Eastern traditions? When Paul wrote of the power of God, he often used the Greek word *energeia*—energy.

Rather than court defensiveness and fear associated with specific words and labels, let us echo Paul's prayer for us: *that the eyes of our hearts would be **enlightened**, that we would know what is the hope of his calling and what is the wealth of the glory of his inheritance in The Holy Ones*,[21] because that inheritance is the kingdom of heaven even now within us.

SEEKING ETERNAL LIFE

Many of us have assumed that the term "eternal life" refers only to something that begins in the next life, after we die. But it's also something we experience here and now.

In the New Testament, only Yeshua offered a direct definition for eternal life: *Now this is eternal life: that they know you, the only true God, and Jesus Christ, whom you have sent.*[22] The word He used for "know" is the same word used for sexual intimacy. The experience of eternal life is knowing our Father and Christ intimately, and only in that knowing can we know ourselves.

So we ask ourselves each day: Am I knowing the Father, and am I knowing Christ? Or am I knowing what someone else taught me about God, thereby putting my faith in that tradition or teaching about God rather than experiencing God?

It seems that most of us have a relationship with our theology and our thoughts *about* God rather than with the Father and the One He sent as the Word, who preexisted the world of words.

You can know all *about* any person, but that doesn't mean you *know* them. Even the demons know about God and it profits them nothing.

You can know *about* an avocado and believe things *about* it by studying it and dissecting it ad infinitum. But you only *know* (as Yeshua used the term) that avocado when you bite into it and taste it. A child can know the Father this way, perhaps more easily than any adult, which may be why Yeshua said we must become like children, even infants, if we hope to experience eternal life in this world.

OUR JOURNEY

It is as Yeshua said in the week leading up to His death and resurrection: *In this world you will have trouble, but have courage because I have overcome.*[23]

We will find great courage in His overcoming as we realize that we are risen *with* Him.[24] So, then, we too have overcome—we just don't *see* or *know* it and so we suffer still.

Think of your life as being in a boat on the troubled seas. The boat represents all that you think will keep you safe. Dark skies block out the sun, winds tear at your face, angry waves rise to sweep you off your treasured boat and send you into a deep, watery grave. And so you cringe in fear as you cling to the boat that you believe will save you from suffering.

But Yeshua is at peace. How can He be at rest in the midst of such a terrible threat? When you cry out in fear, He rises and looks out at that storm, totally unconcerned.

Why are you afraid? He asks.[25]

Has He gone mad? Does He not see the reason to fear? Does He not see the insensitive husband, the cancer, the terrified children, the abuse, the injustice, the empty bank account, the rejection at the hands of friends, the assault of enemies, the killing of innocents? How could He ask such a question?

Unless what *He* sees and what *we* see are not the same. As He said, though seeing, we do not see.

And what does He see? He sees another dimension in which we are complete and safe and glorified, not subject to harm or punishment in any way. He finds rest in the storm and so can we. His question for us is still the same today: *Why are you afraid, oh you of little faith?*

Yeshua shows us the way to be saved from all that we think threatens us on the dark seas of our lives. Only when we, too, see what He sees can we leave the treasured boat that we think will save us and walk on the troubled waters that we thought would surely drown us.

Yeshua came to restore sight to the blind and set the captives free.[26] The sight He offers us allows us to see into the Father's realm—a view brimming with light, seen only through the eyes of Christ.

Our challenge isn't in *becoming* more than we are, because we are already risen with Him[27] and in Him we have already been made complete.[28] Our challenge is to see who we already are and to abide in that identity, each day and each hour.

The old mind cannot see Yeshua's way for this life—true vision requires new sight. The brain cannot understand it—true knowing is of the heart and requires a whole new operating system to process.

To follow Yeshua's way is to let go of this world's systems to see and experience a far greater one—the kingdom of heaven, which is closer than our own breath.

It is to let go of our continued striving to invite Yeshua into our hearts and instead place our identity in the fact that He has already taken us into His heart.

It is the great reversal of all that we think will give us significance and purpose in this life so that we can live with more peace and power than we have yet imagined.

THE BEAUTY OF UNCERTAINTY

The process of transforming the mind from old ways of thinking to new ways is called *metanoia* in Greek: *meta* (to change or go beyond) and *noia* (one's mind or knowledge). This is translated in the King James as "repentance," an old English word that no longer carries the meaning of the original Greek. In the Greek it reads, *metanoia* (transform your thinking), *because the kingdom of heaven is here*.[29] To awaken to this kingdom in which there is no fear, we must become like little children,[30] letting go of our old mind's systems of reasoning.

To be sure, letting go of old thinking (*metanoia*) often feels utterly uncertain to the old mind, which is addicted to what it knows and fears the unknown. For this reason we tend to shrink from transformation and remain in our old way of being.

Think of your old mind as a shore on one side of a lake or a river, and your new, transformed mind as the shore across that river. The only way to reach the other side is through the river of change, which is filled with intellectual uncertainty.

Or think of the process of renewing your mind like stepping out of a boat that you've been told will save you in dangerous waters. Stepping out of the boat will cause some uncertainty and fear because it means letting go of the things that we *think* keep us safe and who we *think* we are. But be sure, it's the only way to find faith to walk on the troubled waters in this life. In doing so, we discover who we *truly* are beyond those troubles.

So we will embrace uncertainty as an invitation into a faith that goes beyond the old systems that enslave us. Only then can we awaken to a new way of being in love, beyond the old way of being in fear.

If others warn us about the dangers of stepping into deep waters, their fear is understandable—following Yeshua often fills the old mind with fear, which is why few enter the kingdom of heaven, as He taught.

Yeshua calls to us now: *Come to me. Trust. Have faith in Me, not in your boat.*

God's promise cannot fail: *If you ask for a fish, I will not give you a snake.*[31]

His Word to us is clear: *Perfect love casts out all fear* and *I am that love.*[32]

To fear that God might punish us for our questions is to vastly misunderstand His goodness. Our Father loves our questions as much as He loves us.

He will not give us a snake if we ask for a fish. He will not lead us into darkness if we ask for the light. Our Father is infinitely gentle and, as Yeshua said, *He is kind to the ungrateful and evil.*[33] Surely, He smiles on us as we humbly seek the truth, however clumsy or unsure our search might seem to ourselves or to others.

I've never met a sixty-year-old who believes all the same things in every respect that he did when he was thirty. Not one. Views on child rearing or love or judgment or the end times or what constitutes a healthy diet or a hundred other issues invariably change. Beliefs change. So let's not be too dogmatic at any age. We might very well be arguing with a future version of our own selves.

Instead, may we extend grace to ourselves and to others and take the journey alongside each other in humility. May we open ourselves up to knowing our Father intimately rather than defending what we think we know *about* Him.

ALIGNMENT

"Alignment" is the word we use for obedience and belief. Belief is defined as a habitual or constant state of trust. To believe in something isn't simply a mental acknowledgement of something's truth, but going into resonance with it and being in accord with it.

In the same way, obedience is a form alignment. It is tuning into something and being in agreement with it, body, mind, and soul.

Therefore, in this book, belief, obedience, and being in alignment are all only different ways to express the same thing. When we align to (believe in, or are in obedience with) the name (the nature) of Christ, we are saved from the troubled seas in this life. In that salvation, we experience the beautiful music of the kingdom.

Think of a radio player that is tuned by turning its dial. Like that receiver, you can be in obedience to, or aligned to, either static or beautiful music. If you are aligned to the low-nature frequency, you experience only the static of the world. But one small turn on the radio dial and you can align to the high frequency of the kingdom of heaven.

True obedience is aligning our hearts and wills with God's heart so that the two are in one accord, and so in resonance as one, just as Yeshua did. *Not my will* (the earthen-vessel self's prescription of what it thinks should be) *but your will* (the manifestation of God's love in this world) *be done.*[34] Anything else is simply the earthen vessel attempting to make sense of a bunch of static.

Yeshua used a different metaphor in the language of the ancient world. *I am the vine, you are the branches; he who abides in Me and I in him* (aligns with and remains in my nature as one with me), *he bears much fruit, for apart from Me you can do nothing.*[35]

To obey God is to align with Him, and prayer is an alignment to God through words of affirmation or request. To align with God is to set our thoughts on the light as a means of being lifted out of blindness and darkness. It is an acknowledgment that the earthen-vessel self can never fix itself. It is a surrender to the divine light of Christ in us, which sings a song of love and peace.

Only in that alignment can our joy be full. Only in that obedience can we walk on the troubled waters of these lives and find peace and a love for all.

Everything we say, do, and think aligns us with blindness or sight, with darkness or light, with fear or with love. Thus, everything is a spiritual practice, whether we are aware of it or not. We are constantly, in every moment, aligning with one way of being or another. The choice is ours to make each moment of each day.

OUR DAILY JOURNEY

Our daily journey now is bringing the *earthen-vessel self,* or *seen self,* or *temporal self,* or *tent self,* or *outer man* (some of Paul's many terms for the body, brain, and personality self) into alignment with our *glorified self* or *eternal self* by taking our attention off the darkness and fixing our eyes on the light of Christ. Keep your eyes fixed on the unseen self, not on the seen self, Paul taught.[36] Doing this with intention for even a little while each day will dramatically change our lives.

Paul called this process "transformation." *Be transformed by the renewing of your mind.*[37] Again, Yeshua called that same process we undergo as we practice truth being "born again." *Unless a man is born again he cannot see the kingdom of heaven . . . But the one practicing the truth comes to the light.*[38]

The eternal self participates in Christ's divine nature.[39] This is *who* we are, eternally true, the new self, as Paul also called our truest identity, which, *in the likeness of God, has been created in true righteousness and holiness.*[40]

Gnosticism made the mistake of calling the earthen vessel an evil creation that was separate from God, and we do not ascribe to this pattern of dualism. Instead we honor our earthen-vessel selves as the physical expression of who we are as we align to our eternal selves.

In aligning to our eternal selves in Christ, we follow Yeshua's practice and surrender our primary identification with the earthen vessel we've always thought of as *me. Unless you hate* (release attachment to) *your life; unless you deny* (release attachment to) *your whole life; unless you take up the cross daily* (let go of your attachment to this life) *you cannot follow me and experience the kingdom of heaven now at hand.*[41]

An attachment, as used in this book, refers to our clinging to something for the meaning and identity it offers us. If we fear losing something, like money or a relationship, it's because we are attached to it.

In the children's book *Gulliver's Travels*, there's an image of Gulliver on his back, tied to the ground by a hundred small strings, each staked into the earth. Together, they keep him bound and immobile. Attachments are like those strings. They prevent us from rising into our true nature in Christ.

Giving up an attachment isn't a renunciation that calls something evil—again, that was the Gnostic error. Rather, releasing attachment is letting go of our desire for something to give us meaning or satisfy our needs. Almost all relationships are formed in deep attachments and so master us. But now we are awakening to a new identity.

As we release our attachments to this life and awaken to our true identity in Christ—as we align ourselves with who our Father says we are—we will naturally find peace and power in the storms of this life. We will naturally begin to love all that He has created, including our bodies, as gifts given to enjoy rather than instruments that enslave us in condemnation and judgment.

Each entry in this devotional consists of a simple scriptural exploration that invites us to the banquet called the kingdom of heaven, which is here and within us always.

Remember that all teachings and guides are like road maps. They have many signposts and markings that point the way, but in the end, they are only a map.

We must each get on the path ourselves and go where the signposts direct us, or that map is useless to us. In the same way, the teachings of Yeshua invite us to leave the shores of our old mind and venture into the river of transformational change to discover the kingdom of heaven, where Christ and true love reign supreme.

Do you remember the parable of the ten virgins? Each was making her way to a great celebration with oil lamps, but five of the ten fell asleep and let their oil run dry. When the time came, these five had no flame to light their way.

The other five could not share their oil with those who had fallen asleep. Why? The simple meaning is plain: we cannot borrow the oil of our neighbor's transformation. Each of us is responsible for our own journey; we best not grow weary and fall asleep or we will miss out on His banquet—the kingdom of heaven—which can be experienced by us today and always.[42]

Also keep in mind Yeshua's parable of the sower. Once a seed of truth comes to us, the old mind spawned by the father of lies can easily snatch it away so that it doesn't take root. If that seed does take root, it can be choked out by the cares and worries of this world.[43]

In the end, our Father, who is far greater than we can possibly imagine, will draw us to Him through His Spirit, even as we are drawn to Him now. In Him, we are far more loved and powerful than we can possibly imagine. The good news we will encounter on our journey is a bright sun that will chase away the dark clouds of our old mind, exposing the stunning truth.

If we were to simplify that truth for a child, it might be described by the following five simple declarations we will call the Five Seals of Truth, even as *He has placed us like a seal upon His heart, like a seal upon His arm.*[44]

THE FIVE SEALS OF TRUTH

THE TRUTH

ONE: God Is Infinite. He is the light in whom there is no darkness. Nothing can threaten or disturb Him. Nothing can be taken away from Him, making Him less than complete, nor added to Him who is already complete. God is good, far more loving and gentle and kind to His children than any earthly mother or father imaginable.

TWO: I Am the Light of the World. Christ is all and in all. I am created in my Father's likeness and glory. I am finite yet already complete, in union with Christ—I in Him and He in me. Nothing can separate me from His love.

THE WAY

THREE: Seeing the Light in Darkness Is My Journey. As I align to God, who is light, I align to who I already am as the light of the world—the son, the daughter of my Father, glorified and flowing with more beauty and power than I have imagined possible. In that light, I am complete.

FOUR: Surrender Is the Means to Seeing the Light. I will only see who I am and thus be who I am as I surrender my attachment to all other identities, which are like gods of a lesser power that block my vision of my true identity and keep me in darkness.

THE LIFE

FIVE: True Love Is the Evidence of Being in the Light. A love that holds no record of wrong and in which there is no fear. A love that flows with peace and joy on earth as in heaven through the power of the Holy Spirit.

SECTION TWO

THE STORY OF REALITY IN THIRTY SIX WORDS

We remember always: any interpretation of Scripture that does not lead us to a love that holds no record of wrong, leads us to something other than Christ.

As discussed earlier, the words we use are primarily signposts that point to our understanding of truth. They make up the story of how we see the world. But all words are limited by our interpretation of them and the interpretations of those humans who came before us. It is useful, then, to hold the meanings of all words with a far lighter grasp than we hold our experience and knowing of God's love.

The story of the Bible is a story that finally leads us to a love that holds no record of wrong, which is the evidence of being in Christ. If our interpretation of words leads us to fear and or judgment, we gladly reconsider the meaning of those words so that we might discover the story of love that Yeshua came to show us.

Even if words aren't that important to you, the story told in these words might be. You may scan this section for the words that catch your attention—mastery of them is not required to enter into the meditations that follow. But in doing so, you might miss an opportunity to reconsider your journey from fear to love in a powerful and transformative way.

We don't have to agree on the story or meaning of these words, nor find certainty in them. They are by no means exclusive, nor exhaustive, nor do they have to replace any other story you've been taught. Hold them all lightly.

The questions they provoke may be as valuable as any clarity they bring.

THE WORDS

1. THE FORGOTTEN WAY: A simple guide that points to the teachings of Jesus, written for Christians, so that we might awaken to who we are in Christ and discover the true love that He said would be the evidence of those who follow Him.[1]

2. GOD: Our Father, who is the infinitely good Creator and Origin of all that is. We personify God as a He, though we know that God is neither male nor female, which are human attributes. In Scripture God is described with both feminine and masculine attributes.[2] Being infinite, God cannot be threatened, disturbed, or compromised. He cannot fear loss, including the loss of us, because He is love[3] and there is no fear in love. He is the light in whom there is no darkness.[4] Being infinite, He is intimately aware of and involved in every aspect of His creation, including each breath we take and every thought we have.

3. US: We are made from the "Word" and "breath" of God, created in His likeness as the light of the world,[5] intimately experienced by God before the creation of this universe.[6] We are glorified sons and daughters of God,[7] manifested in earthen vessels, in the world but not of it, holy[8] and in union with Christ.[9] Christ is all and also in all, and we are included in that all.[10] As such, in our true nature we are the light of the world, we are love, we are peace, we are the righteousness of God in Christ.[11] Anything less is the misperception of our earthen vessels, which still see themselves as separate from God.

4. CHRIST: The Word of God which preexisted before the foundations of the universe and became the expression of God in material form at creation as announced at the beginning of John's gospel. In the beginning was the Word and the Word was with God and the Word was God. All things came into being through Him (Christ), and apart from Him nothing came into being that has come into being. Thus, the Word, or Christ, is that universal aspect of God that is manifest or expressed in creation, the word made flesh. It is experienced by us, in us, through us, and as us as we awaken to our eternal nature, one with Christ. IN CHRIST: Paul the apostle's most common phrase to express our union or oneness with Christ. Paul's claim that Christ is all, and is in all constitutes the long form. In Christ actually means, in union with Christ.12 This is our truest identity. In (union with) Christ, the fullness of deity dwells in bodily form, Paul wrote.13 This is a statement of all that is Christ, manifested in bodily form, i.e. the body of Christ. Us.

5. YESHUA: The Son, fully God and fully human,[14] who came as the manifestation of the fullness of the Christ which preexisted this world. Thus, He is known as Christ Yeshua, or Yeshua the Christ. Son of God though He was, He learned obedience (came into alignment) to His divine nature in Christ through what He suffered during His life as a man on Earth.[15] Though He was once known in material form, we know Him in the flesh no longer.[16] We now know Him in Spirit. Yeshua came as the last Adam, taught all who had ears to hear the way to see the kingdom of heaven within them, and undid what the first Adam did at the fall, bringing justification to all through His death and resurrection.[17] He came to make known the name (the nature) of the Father *so that His love might be known to us* through our alignment to Christ.[18] As we awaken to the truth of our union with the Father in Christ, we discover the love of Christ, which surpasses all knowledge.[19]

6. THE KINGDOM OF HEAVEN: A dimensional awareness and experience of Christ on this plane of existence called the world. Though in the world, the kingdom of heaven is not of it—meaning, not subject to the knowledge of good and evil, which was the fruit of the fall. The kingdom of heaven, like love, is beyond judgment, beyond evil, beyond fear, beyond grievance and malice of any kind. The kingdom is the very fabric of true love, which holds no record of wrong. It can be seen now with new eyes—vision that comes to us as we are born into a whole new operating system with eyes to see light rather than darkness.[20] This kingdom, Yeshua said, is within even the worst of vipers, His term for the Pharisees of His day.[21] Our journey is to see the kingdom while in a world of darkness. For this, we were born. Awakening out of our blindness to love is the journey of seeing the kingdom of heaven.

7. THE WORLD: The world is the system of polarity—meaning, plus and minus, electrons and protons, up and down, good and evil. The world is not evil nor an illusion, as the Gnostics claimed, but that dimension in which both good and evil are experienced. When Paul and Yeshua spoke of the world, they referred to both the physical world and to the religious and philosophical systems of their day, a time when there was no separation between philosophy, science, government, and religion. In this world we will face many storms of trouble, but in our union with Christ we have overcome[22] and are hidden in God with Christ.[23] Our journey is to awaken to who we are in union with Christ rather than who we think we are in the world of polarity.

8. HELL: Hell is the experience of suffering in this age and the age to come. It is darkness, alienated from any experience of divinity. It can be eternal—meaning, beyond the experience of time and space—but it may also be experienced in time and space. We who are in Christ have no thoughts of being alienated from God in the next life. Because of who we are as the sons and daughters of the Father from eternity past, our salvation beyond this life is utterly sure. Our journey now is to transcend suffering in this life by abiding in eternal life through knowing our Father, as taught by Yeshua. Thus we apply Yeshua's teachings to this age as much as to the age to come. In those teachings, we find salvation from the storms of this life, not just a future salvation that none of us has yet experienced nor can until we die.

9. ETERNAL LIFE: Yeshua gave the only direct definition of eternal life in the New Testament when He said, *This is eternal life:* ***knowing the one true God and the One he has sent.***[24] "Eternal" means "beyond time and all polarity," not the elongation of time, which is a construct limited to this dimension. Knowing God is an intimate experiential intercourse of union. *Eternal life* is that experience of Father, Son, and Holy Spirit now, in the eternal realm, which is beyond polarity. It is abundant life experienced as the kingdom of heaven here and now.

10. LOVE: The word "love" in the Forgotten Way refers to the same love Yeshua spoke of when He said to love our enemies, which we call true love, or divine love.[25] It's the same divine love that Paul described as recording no wrong or evil,[26] and that John described when he wrote, *There is no fear in love.*[27] Love is the light that knows no darkness in the same way God, who is love, is the light and in whom there is no darkness.[28] Love is grace, and it is the fulfillment of the law, Paul wrote.[29] True love isn't an emotion, though it may be expressed as one. It's a high state of being, free from the tree of the knowledge of good and evil, which is judgment. Awakening to this love is our birthright, our only true purpose, and it requires a rebirth into an entirely new operating system. As Yeshua taught, new wine (the awareness of Christ) cannot be held in old wineskins (an old mind bound to judgment and blind to love).[30]

11. FEAR: Fear is the absence of love in the same way darkness is the absence of light. Thus, fear, in all its forms, results from blindness to the light. It has only one primary action and that is to call more fear to itself. Anger, malice, anxiety, judgment, grievance, worry, defensiveness, and the seeking of honor are all manifestations of fear. Our greatest fears are the fear of loss and the fear of not being enough. In union with Christ, we are already risen and glorified,[31] but in blindness to that light, our lower nature seeks security through judgment and justifies fear as a means of salvation. Blind to the light, most of us live in fear most of the time, and we project that fear onto others, blaming their behavior for our insecurity. We judge that which we fear, but there is no fear in love, and he who has been perfected in love knows no fear.[32] The fear-based self walks in darkness and is blind to love. So we turn our sight to love and allow all fear to fall away.

12. SEEING: True sight sees the kingdom of heaven with the eyes of Christ rather than with the eyes of judgment or blindness, which shows us only darkness. *The eye is the lamp of the body*, meaning *our perception determines our bodily experience in this life*. If that perception is clear, our whole experience is full of light. If we misperceive, however, we see darkness, as Yeshua taught. And how deep is that darkness.[33] Thus, both the light and the darkness are in the eye of the beholder. In the eyes of Christ, there is no darkness, only light. Being born again allows us to see with the eyes of Christ.

13. BEING BORN AGAIN: One of Yeshua's metaphors for the process of transformation that allows us to perceive the kingdom of heaven now among and within us. As he said, *Unless a man is born again, he cannot **see** the kingdom of heaven*.[34] We are all on this journey each moment of our lives: from blindness to sight, from fear to love. Being born again is the life-long journey from knowing ourselves only as earthen vessels in the world of judgment, to knowing ourselves in the kingdom of heaven as glorified sons and daughters who operate in a love that knows no fear and holds no record of wrong. This journey requires us to let go of the old mind, which is addicted to judgment, and turn to Christ, who alone can save us. *Born again* can also mean joined in Christ as an event, though it serves us to see it as a journey lest we think that we see when we are yet blind to the kingdom of heaven. As Paul wrote, each day we journey, we are closer to our salvation, which comes in our full awakening.[35]

14. EARTHEN VESSEL: Paul's coined term for our physical bodies, which are like vessels through which our eternal, glorified selves experience this world.[36] These vessels only last for a brief time before they return to the ground, scattered by the wind and eaten by worms. They are a beautiful gift, but they are not *who* we are any more than our clothing is who we are. They are *what* we are for a brief moment in time. The earthen vessel includes not only our physical bodies, but also our brains, our personalities, the roles we play as parent, writer, spouse, teacher, man, woman, and so on, all of which Yeshua teaches us to release attachment to on our journey of being born again to experience the kingdom of heaven while in this world.[37]

15. GLORIFIED SELF: Paul the apostle's term for our true identity in Christ. All who were foreknown by God before time eternal have been glorified, he wrote.[38] Synonymous with "eternal self," "holy ones," "risen self," "unseen self"—other terms Paul used to describe all who are in Christ.[39] Yeshua said that He has given us the same glory the Father gave to Him.[40] Thus we are glorified, however blind we may be to that glory.

16. THE LIGHT OF THE WORLD: The divine light (Christ) known in form or earthen vessel (the world). The light came into the darkness but the darkness did not perceive it, John wrote. *While I am in the world, I am the light of the world,* Yeshua said. And to the masses gathered to hear Him: *You are the light of the world but have hidden that light.*[41] We are the light, but we are blind to who we are and so we stumble in darkness. Yeshua came to bring sight to the blind that we might see and align to who we are as the sons and daughters of the Father.[42]

17. OUR INHERITANCE: Our inheritance is the experience of our inherent, glorified self in union with Christ, manifested in the kingdom of heaven here and now. This inheritance is our birthright as the sons and daughters of the Father and became ours before time began as Paul wrote,[43] but we are largely unaware of it. It is never not ours. We "inherit" or take hold of our birthright as we begin to awaken to our identity as sons and daughters of the Father.

18. THE LOST: All among us who are ignorant of their true identity in Christ, regardless of race, religion, or doctrine. We are lost whenever we forget who we are and condemn others for any reason. But we have no fear because, like a good shepherd, Yeshua leaves the fold of those who see and seeks out even the one who is lost in darkness. And God is supremely gifted at finding the lost, not one of whom He is willing should perish.[44]

19. SALVATION: Salvation, to we who know our identity in Christ, is now a journey of finding freedom from fear and darkness in the storms of this life. The world's plan of salvation is to find comfort in relationships, wealth, health, status, honor, and through social bonding in politics, religion, and ideology. Yeshua's plan of salvation is to find peace and love through faith in Christ rather than through faith in the system of fear that still controls this world. Faith in Christ is evidenced by fruit of the Spirit, the greatest expression of which is a love that holds no record of wrong. As to who will or will not enter suffering in the next life, we leave this matter to our Father as we attend to abiding in eternal life now.[45] As Paul wrote, each day as we awaken, we are closer to our ultimate salvation.[46] In this we are passionate about sharing the good news of God's love with all who cross our paths so that they, too, might awaken to that same love. (See *Witnessing*.)

20. TRANSFORMATION: The process of aligning to the light of Christ. Both "transformation"[47] and "awakening"[48] are Paul's terms for the rebirthing process that shows us the kingdom of heaven and brings one into a childlike state of complete trust and reliance on the Spirit of Truth, rather than in the traditions and teachings of man. Sanctification, salvation, the renewing of the mind, and awakening are all different aspects of this same rebirthing process. Unlike *self-help*, which is akin to redecorating a house to make us feel better in that house, *transformation* remakes the whole house from the foundation up and leads to a whole new way of being in the world.

21. METANOIA: The Greek word that means "changing one's mind," or "going beyond what is thought": *meta* (greater or change) *noia* (knowing or mind). Translated as "repent" in old English: *Repent* (change your way of thinking), *for the kingdom of heaven is already here and in your very being.*[49] Metanoia is also the word Paul used for the process of transformation: *Be transformed by the renewing of your mind.* You cannot put new wine (the truth of who we are) into old wineskins (our old way of thinking or minds), Yeshua taught.[50] So we will surrender our old minds (metanoia) and put on the mind of Christ[51] in order to hold the good news of who He says we are as the light of the world.

22. SURRENDER: Our journey of releasing our attachments to this world, including our old identity in blindness, all of our relationships, our clinging to the earthen vessels we live through, and all of our fixations with personal preference. Surrendering our attachments to others and the world is letting go of our expectations for anyone to be other than they are in any given moment. This is done through *agape* love, which holds no record of wrong. Yeshua described this surrender of attachment as "hating" or "denying" our lives, and He emphasized our attachments to family and intimate relationships.[52] Only then are we able to love others and the world. As we surrender and become like a newborn child who does not judge, we experience the kingdom of heaven now at hand and within us, a journey also called being born again.[53]

23. WITNESSING: Witnessing is *seeing*. To be the witness of Christ is to see Him and to see the kingdom of heaven. Witnessing is also sharing our revelation of Christ with others in a love that does not condemn. Witnessing is not sharing a religion, but sharing Christ, because we are to be the witnesses of *Christ*, not the witnesses of what man has said about Him or the doctrines that have been established using His name. In order to share our witness of Christ, we must first experience Christ, because no one can share what they do not have.[54] The blind cannot lead the blind. As many say, everything but firsthand experience is, in the end, only hearsay.

24. THE LAW: The law refers to that system of punishment and consequence found in this world and in the Old Testament, requiring something of us to receive benefit. It's an exchange or barter in which value is determined by a scale of justice. As such, law is the basis for all fear, because fear has to do with punishment and consequence, as written. But the law is weak and useless, and more, it is the power of sin.[55] It only plays its role by showing us its futility so that we might turn to love and grace, which do not require exchange for benefit.[56] Thus, love is the fulfillment of the law, as Paul wrote,[57] because love alone can offer salvation while the law cannot.

25. GRACE: Grace is the free gift of our union in Christ. Zero payment is required for what is free. Grace cannot be measured because we cannot have more or less for free. Something is either free or it is not. To say *I will give you this* (a benefit), *if you give me that* (a prayer or proper beliefs or works) is not offering a free gift but an exchange. This is not grace. There is no such thing as hyper-grace or too much grace: zero times zero is always zero. Our union with Christ is a free gift in grace, which requires nothing in return.[58] Awakening to that gift, however, requires that we see who we are in union with our Father. Awakening is the prerogative of our free will and our journey in this life.

26. FORGIVENESS: To forgive is to let go of all blame and grievance, not only for the benefit of the ones we forgive, but also for our own healing. Forgiveness is the love that releases all offense, without which all else is worthless. To let go of an offense is to release the idea that an offense occurred. If we do not forgive something or someone, including ourselves, then we are enslaved by that which we do not forgive. He who does not forgive *must* judge as a means of justifying his failure to forgive, and that judgment holds him captive. As we forgive, on the other hand, we free ourselves.[59]

27. JUDGMENT: There are two uses for the word "judgment." The first is a form of condemnation. This condemnation is an attack against another and always brings harm to ourselves as much as to those we attack. This form of judgment comes from fear. It was this form of judgment that Yeshua spoke of when He said, "The Father judges no one,"[60] and "Judge not lest you be judged."[61] There is no exception to this rule. It is our judgment that condemns us, not the Father's, nor Yeshua's.

The second from of judgment is the simple issuing of a verdict, such as in a court. It's a decree of a truth over a lie. Yeshua came as a sword of truth to divide truth from falsehood, and as such, He issued His verdicts fairly. He simply spoke the truth, and one of those verdicts was that whenever we condemn another, we condemn ourselves. Another statement of truth is that all are the light of the world.[62] Another is that what we do to others, even the sinners among us, we do to Him.[63] And so it goes, many staggering verdicts of truth that offend the small mind. The final judgment is the end of all falsehood in the universe and so the end of all condemnation, and this is yet to come.[64]

28. LUST: Inflamed desires or craving of the flesh, the most common of which is the need for control and authority at the expense of another. This lust is most often expressed as the amassing of wealth or political power in community and religion. Lust is also expressed as the consumption of pleasures at the expense of honoring our bodies or others' bodies, such as unhealthy eating for pleasure, or sex at the cost of love, or living in prosperity while our neighbor suffers. Love never seeks to gain at the cost of another. Lust is that which seeks gain at the cost of our true selves and others' true selves.

29. MIRACLE: A supernatural shift that breaks the natural laws as perceived by man and restores the kingdom of heaven on Earth. As such, a miracle is the return to truth—anything less is blindness. The great miracle is the opening of our blind eyes to see divinity as our true identity so that we can express true love in that divinity. This awakening to *agape* love is a shift that is impossible outside of Christ. Indeed, apart from Christ we can do nothing,[65] because everything done outside of our identity in Christ is actually nothing. Everything but love quickly leads to suffering. Thus, it could be said that the only true miracle is *agape* love, and that it is everything. All other physical miracles as such are wonderful but only temporal, such as healings that only postpone disease and death because we all die.

30. SIN: Sin is also often described as *missing the mark*, which we call being out of alignment with the light. In other words, sin is blindness to the light. It is all that blocks our sight of union with Christ, that gift given to us before time eternal. *The sting of death* (fear) *is sin, and the power of sin is the law*, as Paul wrote.[66] In other words, sin involves fear, and the power behind sin is the law. *Whatever is not done in faith is sin*, Paul wrote.[67] Contrast this with love. There is no fear in love, because fear has to do with punishment, as written. Thus, sin is all that is in fear, darkness, and law rather than in love, light, and grace. In the broadest sense, sin is the knowledge of good and evil expressed as judgment rather than grace, fear rather than love, darkness rather the light, and its action is to blind us to who we are in Christ. We are all blind to one degree or another, thus John's statement that whoever claims to be without sin only lies to himself.[68] The most common expression of sin is holding a record of wrong. To this extent, most of us live in sin most of the time. But Yeshua undid the power of all blindness, all sin. His death wasn't to satisfy the demands of a vindictive God who demanded punishment, but a re-creative act that nullified the demands of the *flesh* for punishment. In His death and resurrection, He "paid" for sin and made a way for us to see and experience the kingdom of heaven, which is now among and within us, as we align to the light of Christ through a process He called being born again.

31. PUNISHMENT: Punishment is the action of fear expressed by the lower nature against others and ourselves. There is no fear in love because fear involves punishment, John wrote.[69] Fearing loss, needing to prop up and protect ourselves, we often punish others and ourselves and so find ourselves in suffering. In Christ there is no darkness, no condemnation, no fear, and no punishment. Only the law, which is the power of sin, can threaten punishment, and that punishment comes from us. God does punish that which He does not fear, and He fears nothing. Thus it is written, *The Father judges no one*.

32. SELF-RIGHTEOUSNESS: The egoic desire of the flesh that looks to gain standing with God or man through good behavior rather than through the grace of God. It is the insanity of the earthen vessel seeking to elevate itself through its own power rather than awakening to love. Self-righteousness is as filthy rags to God—meaning, useless.[70]

33. MURDER: One of the most common forms of judgment, which is anger. Even as Yeshua taught, the one who is angry with his brother is guilty of murder.[71]

34. GNOSTICISM: A heresy among early Christians who took Yeshua's clear teaching that we must deny our attachment to earthly lives in order to see the kingdom of heaven, and joined it with a Greek philosophy that the body is evil or of no value. Thus, Gnostics claimed, if the flesh is evil, Yeshua could not have come in the flesh. Furthermore, the Gnostics believed that one was saved through a special knowledge, which, ironically, mirrors many contemporary Christians who claim that only their interpretation of Scripture leads to salvation, while all else is heresy and leads to death. We see the error of Gnosticism while following Yeshua's and Paul's teachings to let go of our attachment to the earthen vessel and fix our eyes on our unseen, eternal self in Christ.[72] Today, the term "Gnosticism" is indiscriminately wielded in fear to cut down anything "Eastern" or "mystical," even though Yeshua was both Eastern and spoke frequently about the mysteries of the kingdom.

35. UNIVERSALISM: A false teaching that all paths lead to God. All paths do not lead to God. Most paths, including many within Christendom, lead to suffering and misery in blindness to God, who is the light in whom there is no darkness. Being in Christ is the only way to see the kingdom of heaven at hand. Only God knows the heart, and we leave the question of who is in Christ to Him and Him alone while we follow Yeshua so that we might awaken to His love ourselves. In so doing, we treat all as we would treat Yeshua, knowing that what we do to the least we do to Him.

36. MODALISM: The false belief that God is made up of three parts (Father, Son, and Holy Spirit) who cannot coexist in the same expression at the same time. We can talk of the Father, the Son, and the Holy Spirit as three expressions or aspects of the Godhead, but we believe they are all ever-present and always will be.

THE
DEVOTIONAL

PRACTICING THE FORGOTTEN WAY

*Read each of the scriptures carefully.
If you are tempted to skip them and go straight to the meditation,
please don't. You will miss the heart of Yeshua's teaching.*

1

I CONFORM TO LOVE

Do not conform to the pattern of this world (fear and judgment) *but be transformed by the renewing of your mind. Then you will be able to test and approve what God's will is—his good, pleasing and perfect will.* (His will is agape, love that can only be known as our minds are radically changed.) Romans 12:2, NIV

There is no fear in love; but **perfect love casts out fear**, *because fear involves punishment* (fear is based on a lie that there will be punishment as taught by the old law)*, and the one who fears is not perfected in love* (does not experience the love of God.) John 4:18

In our first meditation in Book One on the Way of Love, we learned that we were born into blindness with the express purpose of seeing the light within and everywhere, a process Yeshua called entering the kingdom of heaven. That kingdom is the kingdom of love in which there is no sight of darkness, no judgment of wrong, no fear.

As we begin the meditations in Book Two, we consider the darkness—the patterns of the world that blinds us to the light—and we see this law at work within us and in the hearts of all: judgment of good and evil, condemnation of what seems to threaten, grievances against perceived wrongs—all of which are forms of fear. We only judge that which we fear, and what is done in fear always calls more fear to itself. Thus, judgment is a self-perpetuating system that feeds on itself.

We live in a world darkened by judgment which is the fruit of the fall. We have embraced the great deception that we are separate from the light. In that deception we are blind, bound by darkness. Succumbing to the knowledge of good and evil, we honor darkness and fear by our repeated acknowledgment of its power to threaten us.

Thus, the prevailing pattern of the world is this pattern of fear.

Ironically, we think our fears will protect us and so we have developed deep attachments to all the devices we believe will save us from punishment in this world, not realizing that by doing so we only perpetuate more fear.

A small example of the fear that controls us might be seen in a cut on the arm. When we judge a cut as something that diminishes us, we are in fear of the harm it does us. Thus, we condemn the cut as being bad. We then find ourselves in suffering by our own condemnation of that cut., and we run about crying "Woe is me, woe is me! I have been cut on the arm!"

Or we might get the same cut on the arm and see it only as a tear in the earthen vessel that we can either choose to repair or not. Instead of fearing it, we might offer it love, holding no record of wrong, and in so doing we are free of suffering, however much pain we might feel.

The difference between these two reactions is vast. The former is in fear, the latter is in love. This doesn't mean we stand in harm's way and throw our bodies in the path of a whip. It means we do not condemn the whip or the man wielding that whip, knowing that doing so only joins with offense.

The question is, do we want to continue living in fear of harm, of enemies, of our thoughts, of our failures, of our loss of money and relationship and health? Or will we resolve today to awaken to the love in which there is no fear?

For thousands of years now, culture and religion have tried in vain to employ fear as a device to save us from the darkness. That fear has become a deep well of darkness that lives in mankind's very psyche.

But we cannot solve a problem with the same consciousness that created it. We cannot fight fear with fear. Only true love casts out fear. And in the same way that fear calls to itself more fear, so too love calls to itself more love.

Imagine if we lived in a state of being that held no fear. We would still use caution to avoid being burned by a flame if we still wanted use of our hand, but we would have no fear of being diminished by the loss of a hand. We would fear no loss of honor, or possession, or wealth, or relationship.

Rather we would be in love, which holds no record of wrong and fears no evil.

We would fear no harm done to us by the actions of others, including those closest to us. We would feel no need to protect our value by demanding our loved ones be a certain way. We would allow the world to be what it wants to be and we ourselves would be the light in that world, offering true love so that they might see that light and begin to recognize it within themselves.

The light is love and that love casts out all fear of evil, of harm, of danger and of dishonor. Then, as Paul wrote, we will know *what is the good and pleasing and perfect will of our Father*, because the perfect will of our Father is always a love that holds no record of wrong, just like His own love for all He has created.

Anything less is the pattern of a world lost in fear. But we resolve to conform to this pattern of fear no longer. Rather, we conform to love.

PRACTICE

Write down any new insights in your journal. Note changes that you have seen in your attitude and experience in this life.

If all that is done in fear creates more fear, and all that is done in love creates more love, then our path is to choose love rather than fear. The first step in doing so is to recognize that much of our lives have been created in fear. Only then can we begin to surrender to love rather than bow to fear.

A fear might be, "If I don't do this, that will happen. And if that happens, I will be seen as a failure." Or, "My husband isn't loving me properly, and so I am diminished."

All negative emotions are ultimately expressions of fear, mostly the fear of loss on some level. Here are some common expressions of fear: resentment, shame, despair, anger, hatred, frustration, anxiety, worry, anguish, hopelessness, powerlessness, loneliness, betrayal, self-righteousness.

With only a little effort, you will find that much of your life is guided by these kinds of fears. Identify three situations with which you've engaged in fear. Write how each situation might appear through the eyes of Christ, seen in love rather than fear. Release the fear and create a new story, expressing words of love toward the one who has offended you. Then you will see how free you already are and the fear will fade.

ALIGNMENT

I release all that I have created in fear, both now and before, and I bless each of those fears with a love that holds no record of wrong. I am the righteousness of God in my union with Christ. I am in this world that accuses me, but I am not of it. I am in the love of Christ. On this day I see that love in the light of Christ, with whom I am one. I am free through this intention and safe in my Father's arms, as I always have been.

2

THE LOVE THAT HEALS US ALL

*You are the light of the world. A city set on a hill cannot be hidden; nor does anyone light a lamp and put it **under a basket**, but on the lampstand, and it gives light to all.* Matthew 5:14–15

Then He will answer them (those who call Him Lord but do not show true love), *"Truly I say to you, to the extent that you did not do it to one of the least of these* (the sinners of his day), *you did not do it to Me."* (Not *as if unto me*, but actually *to me*, i.e., what we do to others we do to Christ.) Matthew 25:45

The glory which You have given Me I have given to them (we have the same glory, one with Christ), *that they may be one, just as* (in the same way) *We are one* (without any separation) . . . *so that the world may know that You sent Me, and **loved** them, even as You have **loved** Me.* (Only as we awaken to and express true love will the world know what love is and awaken to that same love.)
John 17:22–23

*By this everyone will know that you are my disciples, if you **love** one another.* John 13:35, NIV

Today, we return our minds to the light, and we ask, "What and who is the light of the world?" We know that the light came into the darkness but the darkness did not perceive it, and we know that God is the light in which there is no darkness. Furthermore, the light is true love, and even as light knows no darkness, true love records no wrong.

The light, then, is the divine nature of God that shines in the world as love. And in our true nature, we are part of that light.

This is why Yeshua told all those who'd gathered—sinners and prostitutes and destitute alike—*you are the light of the world*. Each of you and all of you are the divine light in this world, in the same way even the Pharisees have the kingdom of heaven within them.

What you do to the least of these, Yeshua said, speaking of the criminals and destitute in His day, *you do to me*. Not *as if unto me*, but actually *to me*.

As we have learned, all who were foreknown by God before time began are glorified. Who, then, was not foreknown? Who, then, is not glorified?

This is not ours to judge. We have a far more pressing concern.

Our challenge is rooted in the fact that we often deny the light ourselves. We have denied our true identity. We have put it under a basket—a false identity—and so stumble in darkness while accusing others of not being in the light.

In following Yeshua's teaching and example, we treat all as the light of the world, however blind we think they are to that light. We cannot be in the light and hold another in darkness. Their state of being is our Father's business; ours is to know that what we do to the least, we do to Christ.

This doesn't make us Universalists. There is only one way to experience the kingdom of heaven now here and that way is through an awakening to Christ.

Today, we return to the light of love that is our true nature as the sons and daughters of God. And as we walk through this day, we will not deny the light of the world we see in all, just as Yeshua proclaimed.

In adapting this attitude, if we err, we do so in favor of love rather than condemnation. In holding another in darkness, on the other hand, we risk being the judge, and as we judge, we judge ourselves. About this, Yeshua was utterly clear.

So we hold all in the light and give permission to all to become aware of the kingdom within them as we see them in that same light. As they awaken to who they are, they, too, can live in the liberation of the light who is Christ, and so live for Christ.

As we love others without holding a record of wrong, we heal ourselves and we heal the world.

Only as we know our glory, as Yeshua taught, will the world know that they are loved in the same way that Yeshua was loved by the Father. Short of this, we are doomed to repeat a powerless history, convincing others to make a claim of faith without leading them out of the same darkness in which we so often still stumble ourselves.

Today, we follow Yeshua and we see the light in all, even though they cannot see it in themselves. And in that love, the whole world is healed.

PRACTICE

Write down any new insights in your journal. Note changes that you have seen in your attitude and experience in this life.

Make a list of all those you hold in darkness, both those whom you know personally and those groups of people you have condemned. Now think of them as your son or daughter. Finally, imagine that they, too, are the light of the world but are blind to it. You wish to help them see who they are as the light of the world so that they can be aligned to Christ and find freedom in the light, yes?

What would you say to that son or daughter who is blind to who they are?

Let this become a new way of sharing the love of Christ with all you meet.

ALIGNMENT

Today, I see all with the eyes of Christ, holding no one in darkness. Today, I see the light of Christ in _____ and I am grateful for them, even though they are blind to who they are. By seeing the light in others, I see the light in myself, as myself, and so I am the light of the world. As I hold myself high, in the light, the love of Christ cannot be hidden, even as a city on a hill cannot be hidden. Through this claim of the light I am healed.

3

I RELEASE THE MASKS I WEAR

If anyone comes to Me (responds to the good news, e.g., Christians) *and does not hate* (release attachment to) *his own father and mother and wife and children and brothers and sisters, yes, and even his own life* (all the masks we cling to in relationship to others and ourselves), *he cannot be My disciple* (cannot follow Yeshua into an experience of the kingdom now present within all).
Luke 14:26

He who loves (has attachment to) *his life loses it, and he who* **hates his life in this world** (releases all attachment to this life) *will keep it to life eternal* (enter eternal life, which is experiencing the kingdom of heaven now at hand and within). John 12:25

No one can serve two masters, *for either he will* **hate** *the one and love the other; or else he will be devoted to one and despise the other. You cannot serve* (align yourself with) *both God and Mammon.*
Matthew 6:24, NHEB

Today, we consider one of the most liberating teachings Yeshua gave to offer us razor-sharp clarity on our journey into true sight. Though our earthen-vessel self sees it as a hard teaching, we rejoice because it leads us to love and peace. As we let go of our attachment to our earthen vessel, a whole new world opens up to us and we find ourselves indescribably happy.

What we think defines us and gives us significance in this life often blinds us to our identity and purpose—glorified beings born blind to first *see* and then *be* the light in the darkness.

But we have placed our identity in our body, our career, our reputation, our relationships, our honor, our material possessions—all that lifts us up in the sight of our earthen vessel.

Think of these as all the masks we wear. They give us value in the sight of others and in the mirrors we construct to show us who we are. When we look the way society wants us to look, we find comfort. When our bank account has the right numbers in it, we find peace. When our partner honors us, we feel loved. When our children obey, we feel power.

None of these is who we are—they are only roles we play in the game called life. All is well until something or someone threatens what we value. Then we cringe with fear and toss and turn at night, wondering what will save us from the loss we fear.

And so we discover that we have placed our faith in our earthen vessel rather than in our union with Christ. We are mastered by life and slaves to it.

As Yeshua taught, we cannot serve two masters. We get to "hate," or let go of our attachment to, one in order to align to the other. If we want to live in love, we have to let go of fear of loss, which is to let go of all our attachments to this world, especially relationships.

We've been trained by life to feel diminished when our spouse leaves us or our loved one behaves in a way we don't want them to. We call it love, but this is the operating system of fear that leaves us in suffering.

We've been trained to wring our hands when illness strikes our child. This is the way of the world that crushes us.

We've been trained to curse the enemy who threatens the security of our land and our nationality and all that we think is ours to protect. This is the historical imprinting that we all bear in blindness and the cause of endless cycles of pain and brutality.

We stand before the mirror and we bemoan our failure to appear as we would prefer to be seen. And on it goes, ad infinitum, an endless homage to the world of polarity bound in the knowledge of good and evil, which is judgment and grievance. Fear, fear, and more fear masters us each day.

In truth, none of these matter much because all spouses die, all children get sick, all countries eventually fall, all bodies wither and return to dust. None of these defines the sons and daughters of the Father, glorified already. But we only perceive our true identity in the kingdom of light as we let go of our attachment to the system of fear and control in which we have placed our hope.

Today, we think of our bodies and all the relationships and the many roles we play as the masks we wear to give us security and meaning in this life. Even if we've come to Yeshua and sing His praises, we cannot see the kingdom of heaven without letting go of our attachment to all relationships and everything else that we think defines us as earthen vessels, just as Yeshua taught.

When we do let go of our attachment to this world, we can begin to truly love (*agape*) it for the first time, needing nothing in return for that love. We can finally begin to love our spouses and others without judging them for failing to be who we want them to be.

Then and only then do we awaken to the love that holds no record of wrong. Tearing off our masks might be painful at first, but then and only then can we find true peace and joy.

PRACTICE

Write down any new insights in your journal. Note changes that you have seen in your attitude and experience in this life.

An easy practice today: Think of the last argument you had with someone close to you. In that disagreement, they surely did or said something that conflicted with what you wanted them to say or do. Perhaps they said something cruel, yes? You had an attachment to their saying nice things to you, and when they failed your expectations by saying something you didn't like, you suffered and felt compelled to defend yourself. This is commonplace and justified by all in blindness.

Make a list of all the expectations you place on someone close to you. Notice how each expectation actually puts you at their mercy to meet those expectations. Write how you would feel if you held none of those expectations. It feels dangerous to the earthen vessel, yes? You will be unsafe, your mind objects. But consider how you would be if you really didn't expect them to be such and such a way, and how free you would then be to love, really love, that one.

Now you are beginning to understand Yeshua's teaching that we cannot experience love unless we surrender all of our attachments.

ALIGNMENT

Today, I bring the expectations I have projected on all of my relationships to the altar of love, and I surrender my need to defend myself from the failure of those attachments. Rather than judge, I offer love without blame and forgiveness instead of defensiveness. In choosing love, I choose freedom, because my safety in truth needs no defense. I know who I am as the one who has come to see, and I choose to see in love today. And so I am free.

4

THE USELESS LAW I NO LONGER FOLLOW

The former regulation (the law of Moses) *is set aside because it was* **weak and useless** *. . . and a better hope is introduced* (the law of grace), *by which we draw near to God* (know Him intimately).
Hebrews 7:18–19, NIV

Wherefore **the law was our schoolmaster** *to bring us unto Christ, that we might be justified by faith. But after that faith is come* (faith in union with Christ), *we are* **no longer under a schoolmaster**.
Galatians 3:24–25, KJV

The Law came in so that the transgression (sin, evil, darkness) **would increase** (the more you try to fulfill the demands of polarity/law, the more failure it brings); *but where sin increased,* **grace abounded all the more**, *so that, as sin reigned in death, even so grace would reign through righteousness to eternal life through Jesus Christ our Lord* (as we see the futility of following the law, we finally surrender to grace and experience eternal life through Christ).
Romans 5:20–21

Do not think that I have come to abolish the Law or the Prophets; I have not come to abolish them but to **fulfill** *them* (by offering love).
Matthew 5:17, NIV

Therefore **love is the fulfillment** *of the law.* Romans 13:10

Imagine that you are imprisoned in a room with brick walls and told since birth that the only way out is to beat your head against those walls until they finally crumble. For years you bang your head, bloodying it over and over, but to no avail. Finally you surrender, realizing that no matter how hard you try, the walls remain immovable.

Only then, in your surrender, do you awaken to the realization that there is an open door right behind you, but your eyes have been so fixed on the brick wall in front of you that you haven't seen it.

The law, which is the system of justice that demands payment, is like that brick wall. And it is indeed a schoolmaster for us, because it teaches us that the harder we try, the thicker it gets and the more we fail (transgression increases, as written). As such, that schoolmaster finally leads us to the realization that our attempt to follow it is useless. It is not our effort that saves us but grace, lest anyone boast in their own efforts.

In grace there is no imprisonment but the imprisonment we have perceived in blindness to the kingdom within us, and it is the law that has blinded us. In grace there is no record of wrong, no brick to dislodge, no barrier that must be overcome. What must be overcome is the illusion that there is a barrier.

In grace there is no price demanded of us, except the cost of letting go of all we thought we were to realize who we are in Christ. And that cost is no cost at all, except to the earthen-vessel self who has made himself a god. Thus, surrendering to grace is harder for the flesh than following the law, even though the law does not and can not liberate anyone.

In coming, Yeshua did not abolish the law; the illusion of freedom through law remains. Instead, He came to fulfill the law—meaning, to finally show its uselessness as a means of any escape from the darkness that has held mankind captive. Indeed, love that holds no record of wrong, rather than judgment, is the fulfillment of the law, as written. And so we now stand in a new law: the law of love and grace, in which we experience eternal life while we walk this earth.

Today, we rest in the law of grace by releasing our binding to the useless law, which has finally brought us, through its failure, to love. Today, we surrender to that love, which knows no record of wrong.

And today we are set free.

PRACTICE

Write down any new insights in your journal. Note changes that you have seen in your attitude and experience in this life.

Take any object and toss it in the air. As far as it travels up, it travels down. This is the law of polarity. In the flesh, all of our efforts to rise are returned with a falling. And so we go, up and down, up and down, round and round. And every harsh word we speak against another is soon returned to us. In this world, we reap what we sow.

But in the kingdom of heaven, the law of grace reigns. There is no down; there is no fear; there is no punishment. Instead, there is the love that does not record wrong.

It is impossible for the natural mind to accept grace, because it must judge others, and accepting grace means it would then have to offer that same grace to others. All efforts to attain godliness and self-righteousness have no power but the power to keep us in blindness and suffering.

Once again we align to the radical love and grace of Christ. Today, speak a word of that love and grace to three people. Tell them how well they are doing, rather than what you think they should do. Tell them how beautiful they are, rather than how to become beautiful. See their eyes light up and write your reflections in your journal.

ALIGNMENT

Today, I offer grace to all I see and to all I meet. Today, I offer love to all I know and all I've ever known. And as I offer this forgiveness, I am forgiven. As I offer this healing, I am healed. In so doing, I am giving permission to all I see with the eyes of Christ to see the light in themselves and in the world. I am the light of the world, and in loving all, I lift that light high to be seen by all. It was for seeing myself as love that I was born; it is for Christ in me and me in Christ that I live. And in this life, I am free.

5
I AM IN THE NAME OF CHRIST

By myself I can do nothing (speaking as Yeshua, the man, not Christ, who can do all things) . . . *I seek not to please myself* (Yeshua, the man) *but him who sent me* (the Father). John 5:30, NIV

Anyone who has seen Me (Christ, who is the Word and the light), *has seen the Father* (because Christ and the Father are in union as one). John 14:9, BSB

As He is (in the same way Christ is right now), **so also are we in this world.** 1 John 4:17

The Father . . . **will give you another Helper** *. . . that is the Spirit of truth . . . In that day you will know that* **I am in My Father** (I am in union with the Father), **and you in Me, and I in you.** (Likewise, you are in union with Me. Knowing our union with our Creator is the primary function of the Spirit. Only then can we bear the Spirit's fruit of love, joy, and peace in this life.) John 14:16–17,20

Believe Me that I am in the Father and the Father is in Me (Christ is in union with the Father) *. . . he* **who believes in Me,** *the works that I do, he will do also . . . Whatever you ask* **in my name,** *that will I do . . . If you ask Me anything* **in my name** (in the identity of Christ), *I will do it.* John 14:11–14

Whatever is asked in His name will be done. We wonder why Yeshua's pronouncement of that simple, universal fact doesn't seem to be our experience. The reason is clear: we aren't believing in His name or asking in His identity. Yeshua did not lie; rather, we have only misunderstood what it means to believe and ask in His name.

The word "name" means the identity or nature that name represents, not the word with three syllables pronounced "Yeh-shoo-uh." Indeed, thousands of people were named Yeshua at that time. The word has no magical power in and of itself. "Name" means "nature"—identity.

So, then, what is His identity and how do we believe in it? How do we ask in that identity?

We believe in the identity of Christ only as we awaken to our oneness with that identity. To believe in Christ is to align to our identity in union with Christ.

If there is one teaching that perhaps best encapsulates all of what Yeshua came to teach, it is found in John 14, above, where in one teaching He directly connected our identity with our staggering power in that identity.

And He made it clear: our identity is found in union with Him.

Where Paul the apostle used direct language to proclaim the great mystery of our oneness with Christ (*Christ is all and in all,* etc.), Yeshua used word pictures as His preferred way of speaking. The word picture He used here is plain, but as written here, it can only be experienced through the Spirit of Truth, the Holy Spirit, whose primary purpose is to reveal our union with Christ to us.

He explained union like this: *Anyone who has seen Me has seen the Father. I am in My Father*—meaning, the Father and I are in union as one. Then Yeshua continued: *And you are in Me, and I am in you*—meaning, in that same way, you are one with Me. He repeated this same teaching in John 17.

This isn't to say that Yeshua, the man, was the Father, because He also said that He, as Yeshua, *could do nothing by Himself.* And that He, as Yeshua the man, *sought not to please Himself, but His Father.* He's drawing a distinction between Himself in flesh and His Father, to whom His earthen-vessel self yields. But Yeshua as the Christ was one with God. He was fully human (Yeshua the man) yet also fully God (Yeshua as the Christ) at the same time.

Whatever we might think of this unfathomable mystery, we see that Yeshua taught us that whatever relationship He had with the Father is the same relationship we have with Him. We in Him and He in us at the same time, just like He and the Father. This doesn't mean we are the Christ, but rather that we are an aspect of Christ, who is manifested through us in earthen vessels. This is the great mystery, as Paul, the greatest of all mystics, called it.

Imagine for a moment a bowl of milk. You see the milk and you see the bowl. Now imagine that Christ is the milk and you are the bowl. The milk is in the bowl, and this is how most Christians think of Christ in them.

But Yeshua went further. The milk and the bowl are in each other, He said. *In the same way that I am in the Father* (as one), *I am in you and you are in Me* (we are one with Christ).

How can the milk be in the bowl and the bowl also be in the milk at the same time? This seems impossible to us. The stuff called *bowl* can't be in the stuff called *milk* and vise-versa, unless the bowl is somehow the same stuff as the milk, unless they are of the same atoms and molecules, unless they are of the same essence and spirit—the same light.

Think of two atoms. We can imagine them very close to each other—touching each other even—but can we imagine them *in* each other at the same time? How can two atoms be in each other rather than just side by side unless they are one? Unless there is absolutely no separation between them because they are in true union?

This is Yeshua's word picture for how we are one with Christ. It is in the same way—just as—He is in the Father and the Father is in Him: two but one.

This is the basis of Paul's declaration that *Christ is all and also in all*.

Some would say, "Yes, we are in union with Christ, but you must not 'collapse' that union." Will we then make it two once more and create separation between the milk and the bowl?

Could it be that the *denial* of who we are in and through Christ is the blasphemy of the Spirit in which we find ourselves cast out and alienated from our identity? Perhaps this is why our faith has proven powerless to show the true love of Christ.

We think in terms of separation, bound by time and space, but Christ isn't limited by space or time. So, then, neither are we, except in our blindness to who we truly are.

Will we be defined by the old mind that holds us in separation from our Father, or will we be defined by Christ, in whom we are one? As we align to who we truly are and ask in that identity, we have great power in Christ.

Our challenge is that we've never learned how to ask in the identity of Christ because we don't see ourselves in that identity. Instead, we tend to ask in our earthen-vessel identity, only *using* the name Yeshua like an incantation, a practice that has failed to prove His universal law that whatever is asked in His identity will happen.

So we ask the Spirit of Truth to reveal the great mystery of our union with Christ to us so that we might awaken to it. And as we begin to awaken to who we are in the identity of Christ, we believe in Christ and we begin to ask in that identity, joined as one, hidden in God with Christ.

Then, we will know who we are.

PRACTICE

Write down any new insights in your journal. Note changes that you have seen in your attitude and experience in this life.

In our blindness, we think we know what we would ask in the identity of Christ, and those things are all that the earthen-vessel self thinks will give it more security and significance in this world. Money, health, beauty, and relationships. But how can we know what we would ask in the name of Christ if we haven't awakened to that identity?

Today, write a prayer to the Holy Spirit, asking your Helper to reveal to you the wonder of the Christ, in whom you are one, just as Christ is one with the Father. This is the ministry of reconciliation, which is the primary function of the Holy Spirit. In that reconciliation, revelation will come.

Then you will know what to ask in His identity.

ALIGNMENT

I set my intention to see in the light by awakening in that light through the power of the Holy Spirit. And in this I will surrender to my Helper, who will lead me in all wisdom and love. Today, I let go of what I think I need so that the Holy Spirit can show me my identity in Christ. In that identity, I will know that I need only Him. In that identity, I will know that I am already complete and need nothing but the experience of my completeness in Him.

6

I COME LIKE A LITTLE CHILD

Truly I tell you, unless you change and **become like little children**, *you will never enter the kingdom of heaven.* Matthew 18:3, NIV

At that time Jesus said, "I praise You, Father, Lord of heaven and earth, that You have hidden these things (the mysteries of God) *from the wise and intelligent* (human theology based on reason and law) *and* **have revealed them to infants**.*"* Matthew 11:25

Again and again Yeshua likened the transformation we experience to starting all over, stripped of the history and the reasoning that we think defines us in this world.

Unless you become like infants, you cannot enter or experience the kingdom now at hand. The Father reveals the mystery of truth to infants while it remains hidden from our raw human intelligence, Yeshua taught. No one is special in awakening to this mystery—that was the Gnostic fallacy. Rather, we simply awaken to our natural state of being as the sons and daughters of our Father.

Reasoning and analysis are the prerogative of beta waves in the human brain. Without beta waves, there is no mechanism for reason or logic. It is now known that the brains of infants hardly use beta waves for the first year. They learn through experience rather than through reason and analysis.

Revelation comes through firsthand experience of God rather than through intellectual ideas, which become dogma.

The fact that intelligence is not required always frustrates the intelligent mind. Infants trust without human logic. Through being transformed by the renewing of the mind, or being reborn like an infant, we awaken to revelation. As also said by Yeshua: *Unless one is born again* (becoming like an infant) *they cannot **see*** (perceive) *the kingdom* (which is already here and everywhere).

Seeing beyond the judgment and human reasoning that characterize this world of darkness requires letting go of the reasoning we once clung to and stepping into a whole new way of being. It's as if we were being born all over again without the old mind that we depend on for meaning and survival.

We now see that various words in English describe this process. *Sanctification, transformation, awakening, being born again, enlightenment, alignment, purification*—all these are different sides of the same gold bar. At the very least, it perhaps serves us best to think of them as the same process, lest we get caught up in minutiae that divide us.

An infant doesn't see herself as separate from her mother for the first year of life. Can we see ourselves in the same way in our relationship with God?

An infant depends on and trusts his mother implicitly, innately experiencing love as his natural state of being. An infant cries at pain and in alarm, but it doesn't know how to condemn or judge.

An infant is *childlike*, full of simple trust and in union with her source. Spoiled children, on the other hand, can be *childish*, spoiled by their own demands and desires.

Today, we allow ourselves to be born again like an infant. In so doing, we will be childlike, surrendered to our Origin, rather than childish and so yielding to our earthen vessel's judgments and demands.

Today, we see the world with the innocence of a small child and we are free from all the cares and concerns that have haunted us as if they never happened.

And in that transformation, we see the kingdom of heaven within us.

PRACTICE

Write down any new insights in your journal. Note changes that you have seen in your attitude and experience in this life.

The world we live in is childish in its ways of judgment, throwing fits over those who disagree and cowering in fear when the dark storms rise. But we set our heart on being childlike, not childish.

Imagine today that you are a child. That young you has come to the you who sits reading this meditation, and she's come seeking assurance and love from you.

Minister to your childlike self by offering her truth and compassion when she is confused or in pain. Write down what you would say to him in need of a mother's love. If you like, address a particular situation that might be causing fear. Be tender and loving, because all children know love when they encounter it.

ALIGNMENT

Today, I will be like an infant in union with her mother, with his mother, receiving care and love. I am loved without condition. I am accepted and treasured, without the faults that others might frown at. I am one with my mother and with my Father. No harm can come to me in the arms of love. I am whole. I am complete. I am loved and one with them. I am free.

7

I AM GRATEFUL FOR MY STRUGGLES

We also glory in our sufferings because we know that suffering produces perseverance; perseverance, character; and character, hope. And hope does not put us to shame, because God's love has been poured out into our hearts through the Holy Spirit, who has been given to us.
Romans 5:3–5, NIV

And we know that all things work together for good to them that love God (those who are in alignment with divinity see that nothing can compromise Him or them), *to them who are the called according to His purpose* (the sons and daughters of the Father).
Romans 8:28, KJV

*He **has made everything** beautiful in its time. He has also set **eternity** in the human heart; yet **no one can fathom** what God has done from beginning to end.* Ecclesiastes 3:11, NIV

Trust in the Lord with all your heart and do not lean on your own understanding. Proverbs 3:5

In this world we will have trouble and face many storms. We who know that we were born blind for the express purpose of seeing the glory of our Father displayed inside of us and in all creation can see that all these struggles are working for good.

Consider a star that burns out and explodes in a supernova. It is said that supernovas are now the engine of all planetary formation. As a star, which is comprised mostly of hydrogen, burns out and collapses in on itself, it generates incredible forces and heat, and in that pressure cooker, the dying star creates iron and then all of the heavier elements, including gold. In 2017, astronomers witnessed and measured, for the first time, the formation of all the elements that make up our planet in such a supernova. When the star explodes, all those elements are scattered into space and eventually are pulled together by gravity to form new celestial formations.

Gold in all of its beauty is formed in a fiery furnace of great cataclysm. You might say a star goes through terrible suffering to produce such beauty.

In the same way, we see that all things are working for good in our own lives, even when the storms seem to be tearing us apart.

We can think of those storms that refine and heal us as the wrath of God, if we like. Wrath is not anger expressed at something, but love that removes what harms us. It is a beautiful process that delivers us to the hope of our calling—the experience of the kingdom within us. It is for this we were born.

When a mother wipes the puss from the infected eyes of her small child, does the child's crying mean she is being cruel to her child? What might seem like calamity to the child is for his own good and healing. So it is with God's wrath. How loving and gentle is God as He heals our blindness and shows us the light.

Some have said that all things work out for the benefit only of those few who are special and love God at the expense of everyone else, but this interpretation leaves all wondering if they are those few who truly love God. Do not all yet struggle with their sin nature? Who then is special, claiming they are without sin?

Rather, we see that our Father is infinite and works out all things according to His love and purpose, and He cannot fail to fulfill those purposes.

So we trust our Father. And although we cannot fathom what He has done from beginning to end, we trust that He has made everything beautiful in its time, as written. Therefore, we are thankful even for our struggles, which lovingly lead us to the full realization of who we are and of the love that is native to our truest selves, risen with Christ.

PRACTICE

Write down any new insights in your journal. Note changes that you have seen in your attitude and experience in this life.

Learning to trust that God has already made everything beautiful in its time is impossible for our natural minds and requires an alignment to our Father through a knowing of Him personally rather than through what is written about Him. As you surrender to trust rather than leaning on your own understanding, you will find peace in the storms of this life.

Think of something that you might have once seen as the punishment of God in your life. Journal about it through a new lens, seeing it not as punishment but as a beautiful gift of simple love inviting you to rise into the light of your true nature. See the past in that new light and let it heal your mind. You were born blind to see in darkness. See the light in the darkness today and be healed.

ALIGNMENT

I release all that I once thought harmed me, and in surrendering my own old understanding, I trust in God, the Infinite One, who has already made everything beautiful in its time. In surrendering to the light, I bring glory to what I once cursed, I offer gratefulness for what I once feared, and I lift my eyes in wonder of the One who works all for good in my life. Like a child, I trust my Father. And like that child, I abide in His love, which holds no record of wrong. In this love, there is no fear of the past, or of the present, or of anything that might come to pass. In the love of Christ I am free.

8

I LEAVE THE OLD BEHIND

No one can serve two masters (two systems) *for either he will hate the one and love the other; or else he will be devoted to one and despise the other. You cannot serve* (align yourself with) *both God and Mammon* (the system of the world). Matthew 6:24, NHEB

If (since—rhetorical) *you have died with Christ to the elementary principles of the world* (polarity, law), *why, as if you were living in the world* (attached to the world), *do you submit to decrees, such as, "Do not handle, do not taste, do not touch!"—which all refer to things destined to perish with use* (the useless law)—*in accordance with the commandments and teachings of men?* (The law is weak and useless, yet still embraced by man.) Colossians 2:20–21

In the same way, those of you who do not give up everything you have (all of your attachments to this world) *cannot be my disciples* (cannot follow me into an experience of the kingdom of heaven, which is light and love). Luke 14:33, NIV

Since, then, you have been raised with Christ (since you are spiritual beings in union with Christ), *set your hearts on* **things above where Christ is, seated at the right hand of God** (the kingdom of heaven here and now). *Set your minds on things above* (life in Christ; love), **not on earthly things** (earthen-vessel life; law). *For you died, and your life is now hidden with Christ in God.* Colossians 3:1–3, NIV

There are two systems at play in this world of polarity. The first is the system of the law, constructed from the fabric of fear and control. According to this system, if the appropriate payments are not made, we will be diminished, so we must honor payment. This is the system of exchange, where what is received requires a price of some kind. We pay money; we receive goods. Thus money, or mammon, is the symbol of the entire system of fear and control. We will call this the system of the world.

The other system is the system of love and grace, which requires no payment for reward, offers no grievance for what was done, and keeps no record of wrong. We will call this system the kingdom of heaven.

We hear of the kingdom and we so long to be in that state of being even while we once cringed in fear. But although our sight of that kingdom comes, it seems to vanish as quickly as it came.

And the reason is clear to us as we hear Yeshua's teaching. *You cannot serve two masters at the same time.* Our challenge is that we always run back to the old way of being because we have invested in the false security of that way for so long.

Imagine being in a room—a beautiful basement apartment. This room is your life, your possessions, all your relationships, all that makes you who you think you are and gives you value. It's a room adorned with equal amounts of comfort and fear, because everything that gives you comfort must be protected for fear of loss. And you know that one day the room will be taken from you, so you fear that death as well.

Truly, the more you have, the more that will be taken from you. And so you live in fear of loss. The husband will cheat; the child will die; the car will be repossessed; the beautiful face will wrinkle; the insecurity behind your mask will finally be exposed for all to see.

But there is a staircase and a door to another room above. Christ is that door. Beyond the door is a whole new world—a dimension of light and wonder, love and beauty. But it's also a place that doesn't guarantee all of the securities that you've leaned on for so long. It's full of mystery beyond all the ways you've known yourself thus far.

Do you want to enter the experience of this kingdom of heaven?

The only way to enter the new room above is to leave the old room behind. You cannot serve both rooms at the same time. You cannot have two masters.

Our challenge is that we often place one foot in the new room and speak of its wonders, but then quickly withdraw into our old securities. Or we try to stand with a foot in each room and wonder why we don't experience love as it was promised.

As written, we must align with the world above where Christ is rather than to lower things, which is the earthen vessel's native nature.

We must leave one room to enter the other. We can only enter the kingdom of heaven at the cost of the old way of being in this world. But we value our old way of being so highly that we turn from that door and return to our little treasures that moth and rust destroy.

As we walk into the room called the kingdom of heaven, we discover that it's actually a whole new dimensional perspective of the old room. In that perspective, the old room is made new. All is in love. All is in light.

Should we enter the kingdom of heaven today and find great joy?

The only way is to leave the old room.

PRACTICE

Write down any new insights in your journal. Note changes that you have seen in your attitude and experience in this life.

There is no accusation or condemnation in today's practice, because we are all born blind to experience the light. Rather, we accept an invitation to see why we keep struggling to find love in the old room, when it can only be found in the new room. In that new room, we find ourselves, because we are already risen in Christ. In the old room, we continue to search for ourselves where we cannot be found.

Think of your life as a room filled with what you value today, and imagine what it would be like to see every object and person from a new perspective. Condemn nothing, but see it in the light. In that love, you may appreciate what you see, but you need nothing.

What are you clinging to that keeps you from stepping into the room that needs nothing but its own light? Do not condemn yourself, only observe. Now speak a blessing over all that you see, drawing it into light rather than condemning it for its failure.

ALIGNMENT

Today, I offer love to all that I see before me. I release everything that I cling to in this world for security and meaning to the light of Christ as I step into my inheritance as the son, the daughter of the Father. I ask the Spirit of truth to bring new sight, that I might see with the eyes of the Christ. And in doing so, I am free from all that would keep me bound to the old way of being in the world I live in. I am love, I am light, I am the child of my Father, and all He has is mine.

9
MY NEW OPERATING SYSTEM

*No one pours new wine into **old wineskins** (old operating system). Otherwise, the new wine will burst the skins; the wine will run out and the wineskins will be ruined. No, **new wine must be poured into new wineskins** (new operating system). Luke 5:37–38,* NIV

I am the vine, you are the branches; **he who abides in Me and I in him, he bears much fruit** *(love),* **for apart from Me you can do nothing** *(all is vanity in the earthen vessel alone) . . . My Father is glorified by this, that you bear much fruit, and so prove to be My disciples. Just as the Father has loved Me, I have also loved you;* **abide in My love**. *(Love is the greatest of all fruit, the evidence of Christ.)* John 15:5,8–9

If you try to put new wine in old wineskins, the old wineskins will rupture. In the same way, if you try to put new revelation into an old way of being, that old way will only spoil the new revelation. Rather, only a new mind will be able to hold new revelation.

Two thousand years ago, Yeshua used analogies that would be understood by an ancient people. Today, we use a new analogy that mirrors His.

Let's imagine that a wineskin is the programming for a computer operating system. You can't run Apple programs on a Microsoft computer, we might say. If you want to run Apple apps, you need a whole new operating system—namely, an Apple operating system.

Our first challenge is that we often try to import the new way of love into old systems of fear and control, and the system crashes. This is what happened when Christianity returned to the law in the centuries following Yeshua's death. Despite Paul's warning not to return to the law, we did, calling the system "Christianity," yet stripping it of grace and love found in union with and participation in Christ.

How many wars have been fought under the banner of that Christianity? How many people were burned at the stake for heresy? And how many are still burned at the stake of condemnation today?

But now we awaken to the new wineskin, which is a new operating system called love and grace, crafted in the fabric of our union with Christ, which is the opposite of the world's way of judgment and grievance bound to the knowledge of good and evil.

As we abide in the vine of new wine, which is the revelation of Christ in us, our lives bear the fruit of the Spirit: true love, true joy, and true peace.

Above all, love, which proves the truth of His power to transform our lives.

Indeed, apart from Christ we can do nothing, because everything we do in the old operating system—the old wineskin—will finally be shown to be nothing more than dust returning to dust, so nothing at all.

Life is found only in Christ. Truth is found only in Christ.

We abide in the vine of Christ today.

PRACTICE

Write down any new insights in your journal. Note changes that you have seen in your attitude and experience in this life.

The truth is, we are already hidden in God with Christ. We are already glorified and in the light; we do not know darkness or fear. We are only blind to that light and so continue to live in the old wineskin.

The old operating system uses fear to protect itself from crashing. The operating system of love knows no fear. The old judges and condemns as a means to make itself safe; the new forgives and loves all it encounters and can never be compromised.

Make note today of the old patterning of thought you return to over and over, seeking security. Now let the love of Christ cleanse those fears and insecurities through the cleansing water of the Holy Spirit.

ALIGNMENT

You are the vine and I am the branch, and as one we produce love, peace, and joy. Today, I lift all of my old patterns of thought and beliefs into the light of love and grace, which is my inheritance in Christ. In that light I am free from fear, free from worry, free from depression and loneliness. In that light I am healed and I am complete. Nothing can harm me because I am who my Father says I am and who I now know myself to be: one in Christ.

10

I HAVE EARS TO HEAR

*(You) have put on the new self **who is being renewed to a true knowledge** (our awakening is a journey of renewal) according to the image of the One who created him (into the truth of our union with God revealed by the Spirit)—a renewal in which . . . Christ is all, and in all.* Colossians 3:10–11

And that from a child you have known the holy scriptures (the Old Testament) *which are able to make you wise to salvation through faith which is in Christ Jesus. All scripture* (the Old Testament) *is given by inspiration of God, and is profitable for doctrine, for reproof, for correction, for instruction in righteousness.*
(The Old Testament is profitable even as it shows us failed views of God, which lead us to grace. Often Yeshua quotes God in the Old Testament, e.g., *You have heard it said "An eye for an eye,"* and then He overturns what God said with a teaching of love and grace: *But I say do not resist an evil person.* In essence, much of the Old Testament shows us how not to live.) 2 Timothy 3:15–16, AKJV

As for you (followers of Yeshua), *the anointing which you received from Him abides in you, and **you have no need for anyone to teach you**; but as His anointing teaches you about all things, and is true and is not a lie, and just as it* (the Holy Spirit) *has taught you, you abide in Him.* 1 John 2:27

He has made us competent as ministers of a new covenant (grace and love in the power of the Spirit)—*not of the letter* (what is written as

Scripture) *but of the Spirit; **for the letter kills, but the Spirit gives life**.* 2 Corinthians 3:6, NIV

Each of us asks ourselves today, "Do I trust the Holy Spirit to speak to me, or must I put my trust in what man has said about what the Holy Spirit told them? And if I must put my trust in man rather than in the Holy Spirit, which man must I trust? So many have said so many different things."

Consider this: We have learned that Christ is all and in all, which includes us. We have learned from Yeshua that this great mystery will be revealed to us by a helper—the Holy Spirit.

But can we hear the Spirit?

Consider this: Yeshua taught that we must become like little children because the Father reveals Himself to children and hides Himself from the intelligent.

But can we become like little children to hear revelation?

Consider this: We are one with Christ, and that one, our truest identity, lives in and through our earthen vessel. So, then, our truest self is also joined with the Holy Spirit. But can we hear our true self, who already knows the truth?

We must confess and say, not very well most of the time, yes?

Perhaps it's because we have put our faith in the opinions and interpretations of others for so long that we have deafened our ability to listen for, much less hear, the Spirit of Truth. Do we put our faith in this book or in what others say about a letter written by Paul two thousand years ago?

Our faith is in God alone even as we trust that Paul's letters were inspired by God and point the way to finding ourselves in Christ.

Only the Spirit gives life; only the Word who is Christ divides truth from falsehood. The written letters cannot, because they are subject to vast swings in interpretation according to the traditions and languages of mankind.

As Paul wrote concerning the Old Testament *the letter kills but the Spirit gives life*. And this surely extends to all of that which is written. Thus there is no end to arguments and accusations of heresy and division among those who claim to know Christ. Truth comes from the Word of God and that Word is Christ, revealed to us by the Holy Spirit.

And yet many of us are truly afraid to listen to the Spirit, leaning instead on what we have been taught *about* God by those who came before us.

Consider a peach. Imagine studying that peach under a microscope and writing volumes on its every detail. A hundred scientists join you, all donning white coats and wearing little golden peach pendants to signify their identity as knowers of the peach.

But do you and they *know* the peach? No, you only know *about* it. A child can walk into the room, pick up the peach, take a bite out of it, and *know* the peach rather than just *knowing about* it. And she likely won't have words other than "sweet!" and "I love it!" to explain her knowing.

That peach is like God, whom we may taste to see His goodness. *Taste and see that I am good*. That peach is also like the Scriptures. Our journey is to taste and know rather than simply study and know about. Only then can we discern the truth behind those apparent discrepancies that arise in what is written about God.

Case in point: deep within, we know that much of what some have been taught about a hateful and punitive God must certainly misrepresent our Father, because it wages war against both the teachings of Yeshua and the love that we experience in Christ—a love that is neither provoked nor holds a record of wrong.

What then is more true? Our deep awareness of the goodness of God, or the traditions of man and scholars who teach a punitive

Father who demands an eye for an eye, and taught that opinion to our parents, who then taught it to us so that we can teach it to our children?

We know this: for generations, fear has put us in bed and tucked us under its dark sheets, promising to protect us. *Be afraid, very afraid, because you might be wrong and suffer deeply. Be afraid and do not trust in your hearing. Listen only to me because those who listen to the Spirit are led astray!*

But the Holy Spirit, like a loving mother, never speaks fear into the child. Instead the Spirit whispers love and kindness and magnificent goodness of the Father.

Who then do we listen to? As John wrote, *We have no need that any man teach us.* Rather, we learn to hear the Spirit of Truth, who will help us awaken to the truth of our union with Christ.

The news is better than we could have imagined! Fear is the cruel voice of the accuser bound to law, not the sweet song of the Spirit that washes over us in grace. Any interpretation that doesn't lead us to a love that holds no record of wrong leads to something other than Christ. We follow the example of the Spirit, who loves us like a mother who holds no record of wrong in her infant child.

All children know a good story when they hear one, and it's time for us, as the children of God, to begin hearing His good story, spoken into our hearts by the Holy Spirit.

This doesn't mean we undermine the written letter we call the Bible—not at all. Instead, like Paul, knowing that the letter does indeed kill and the Spirit indeed gives life, we open our ears to the Spirit so that we might better hear what is meant by what is written. We do this rather than trusting what some other scholar or institution or denomination has said about their interpretation of what was written.

To this end, we become like little children, yielding our hearing to the Spirit's gentle voice, which shows us our blindness and teaches us to see light in the darkness and to accept love in a world of fear. Today, we let all confusion go as we hear the good news that our Father loves us in the same way He asks us to love others: without holding a record of wrong or condemnation.

This is the story all little children know is true. May we have ears to hear the truth in that story.

PRACTICE

Write down any new insights in your journal. Note changes that you have seen in your attitude and experience in this life.

Sit in silence for a minute and try to hear sounds that all the distractions of thought and noise hid from you only a moment ago. What do you hear? Subtle sounds suddenly come into focus. Can you hear them?

Now ask the Holy Spirit to give you ears to hear the simplest story of your Father, of yourself, and of why you are in the world. Hear the gentle voice that whispers to your heart. Speak out the first thoughts that come to your mind.

If the good news of who we are cannot be explained to a child in just a few minutes, perhaps it's missing the goodness of the story. Write the simple story that rose within you in just a few paragraphs, as if telling it to a little child. Tell that little child who their Father is, who they are, and why they are here in this world.

ALIGNMENT

Like a child who is learning to hear her mother's words and see her mother's way, I surrender to the voice of the Spirit today. Although the world has taught me lies about who I am, I release those lies and I listen to the truth I hear from the Spirit of Truth. In that truth, I am free from all the empty philosophies according to the traditions of man that have held me captive, and I awaken to the love of my Father, in whom I am one. In this I hear what is true, and in this I am safe.

11

I LIFT MY EYES AND SEE A NEW WORLD

Say not ye, There are yet four months and then cometh harvest? Behold, I say to you, **lift up your eyes** *(change your perception), and look on the fields, for they are white* **already** *unto harvest. (The kingdom is beyond time, cause and effect. This is the basis for all that is miraculous, seen in the Spirit.) John 4:35,* KJV

The harvest is plentiful (already ripe) *but the workers are few* (few see this). *Ask the Lord of the harvest, therefore, to send out workers into his harvest field* (Yeshua's invitation to be a co-laborer who sees the kingdom of heaven now). Matthew 9:37–38, NIV

For the gate is small and the way is narrow that leads to life (the kingdom of heaven), *and there are few who find it.*
Matthew 7:14

Truly I say to you, whoever says to this mountain, "Be taken up and cast into the sea," and does not doubt in his heart, but believes that what he says is going to happen, it will be granted him. (Yeshua's great teaching on the power inherent in the beliefs of all mankind.) Mark 11:23

Once again we return our thoughts and intentions to the problem of misperception that shows us a dark world. It is as Yeshua said: our perception determines the life we will have in our bodies. *The eye is the lamp of the body.* If our perception is clear, our whole earthly experience in the body will be full of light. If we misperceive, we will see darkness—and how deep is that darkness.

Now He teaches through another metaphor for perception. We imagine Him stopping by a newly planted field of wheat with His followers and pointing.

"You have historically been taught that it takes four months for this wheat to grow and ripen before it is harvested, but that's only your perception based on what you've learned from those who've come before you. I say, lift your eyes, change your perception, and you will see that the wheat is already ripe for harvest!"

Only our faulty perception shows us a linear progression of events bound in the knowledge of good and evil, ripe and unripe, time and space. As we see with the eyes of Christ, we will see that the kingdom is already at hand and within our very being, beyond space and time.

We are not linear beings but dimensional beings. Our journey is to awaken to who we are in the kingdom of heaven. To this end we were born and born blind.

This is the basis not only for true sight but also for all that we would call miraculous, beyond the laws of space and time. The miraculous is simply an alignment to a higher dimension through new sight, and the greatest of miracles is awakening to our true identity in that dimension that Yeshua calls the kingdom of heaven.

Our faulty perspective is what limits us in this world. We believe it will take four months for the harvest to ripen, and so it does. But if we lift our eyes—if we change our perception and truly see it as done—even a mountain can be cast into the sea. This is the power of the sons and daughters of God. But we have been blind to who we are.

So, then, Yeshua calls for us to enter the kingdom of heaven by lifting our eyes—changing our perception and aligning to the light. He said few would follow His way, and few have, but now we ourselves awaken to the harvest and see with the eyes of Christ.

And as we are witnesses of that great light—as we see the kingdom of heaven within us—we give permission for all to also see the light of the kingdom within themselves as well.

And so the whole world is healed.

PRACTICE

Write down any new insights in your journal. Note changes that you have seen in your attitude and experience in this life.

Our powerlessness in blindness has given rise to whole doctrines that seek to justify or explain that powerlessness. Some say Yeshua's teachings were for a different age. Some say that those who first followed Yeshua were special and given the power to experience the miraculous.

You might point to those who pray for miracles and say it rarely works for them, but what if their power is weak because they themselves are still attached to the earthen vessel, holding grievances against illness and being desperate for reward?

What if we were to follow both Yeshua's and Paul's teachings to release attachment to our lives and instead fix our eyes on our union with Christ? What if we were to ask without grievance or fear or attachment to the outcome?

Today, identify an issue you have with your body and offer it love without grievance for being anything other than it is. This is offering it love without holding a record of wrong. Forgive your body and ask the power of Christ in you to make it whole. See it as whole without holding a record of wrong against it.

Do you see how this feels very different from the past ways in which you have condemned your body and begged God to heal it? Write a new prayer for yourself, or for anyone you know who is ill.

ALIGNMENT

In Christ, the harvest is ripe. In Christ, the mountain is moved. In Christ, I am healed, because in Christ I see myself as whole, regardless of what my body tries to tell me. It is me, risen with Christ, who speaks to the mountain, and it is me, glorified in Christ, who forgives. As I forgive my body, I offer it love and lift it to the kingdom of heaven. I love my body without holding a record of wrong. And in this love, I am free of all that I once thought imprisoned me. I speak these words in the name of Yeshua, the Christ, in whom I am one.

12

I AM IN PERFECT PEACE

But God, being rich in mercy, because of His great love with which He loved us, even when we were dead in our transgressions (before we had eyes to see), *made us alive together **with** Christ . . . **and raised us up with Him, and seated us with Him in the heavenly places*** (in the higher dimension) *in* (union with) *Christ Jesus.* Ephesians 2:4–6

They (we) **are not of the world, just as** (in the same way) ***I am not of the world.*** (We are spiritual beings, *in* the world but not *of* it.) John 17:16, BSB

Through these (God's light and truth) *he has given us his very great and precious promises, so that through them you may **participate in the divine nature*** (our state right now), ***having escaped the corruption in the world*** (the knowledge of good and evil) *caused by evil desires* (caused by the desire to be separate from our true nature in union with our Father). 2 Peter 1:4, NIV

*Therefore from now on **we recognize no one according to the flesh*** (literally: the body made of flesh)*; even though we have known Christ according to the flesh* (when Yeshua was alive), *yet now we know Him in this way no longer.* (Because Christ isn't in what we think of as flesh. He is in some form that isn't limited by time or space. Paul called this a glorified body.) 2 Corinthians 5:16
As He is (in the same way Christ is right now in Spirit), ***so also are we in this world*** (so are we, joined as one with Him as Spirit). 1 John 4:17

We ask ourselves these questions today: How is Christ in the world right now? How is He being at this very moment? Is He upset or disturbed, or is He in peace and love?

These are important questions because *as He is, so also are we in the world* right now—not our earthen vessels, naturally, because we regard no one according to the flesh any longer, including ourselves. We are all spiritual beings temporarily living as earthen vessels because, as Paul wrote, everything that can be seen with the eyes, including the earthen vessel, is temporary, but what is unseen is eternal. We are in the world but not of it. Our journey is to align to who He says we are, and so be who we are while still in these earthen vessels.

Yeshua is risen. And so are we, because we are risen *with* Him, as written.

Yeshua is established or seated in union with God in the dimension unseen by natural eyes called the kingdom of heaven. And so are we, because we are seated *with* Him, as Paul wrote. *As He is, so are we.*

Today, we again rejoice in our true identities as those foreknown, established as sons and daughters, and glorified by our Father before time began. And though we were born blind and live *in* this world of polarity in order to see ourselves as the light in the darkness, we are not *of* this world. We are spiritual beings temporarily *in* this world.

If Christ is risen and glorified, and if we are risen and glorified with Him, then we share in His divine nature, as Peter wrote. None of the sufferings we experience in the flesh define us.

Christ is in perfect peace. And so are we, though we are often blind to our glorified selves, seated with Him in that perfect peace. As we align to our true selves in Christ, we find that peace.

Christ is the light of the world who offers grace and staggering love to all of life. And so are we, one with Him. As we align ourselves to that light, we find love.

As we awaken to who we are as the glorified ones, the fruit of the Spirit, which flows with love, joy, and peace, will be our offering to our earthen vessels and to the whole world.

PRACTICE

Write down any new insights in your journal. Note changes that you have seen in your attitude and experience in this life.

As humans, we almost always re-create out of our memory of our history and the programming that has been imprinted on our minds. In our journey of awakening, we still so often try to pour new wine into old wineskin. This simply doesn't work.

Imagine that you just arrived on this planet in the body you now occupy. You have no memory of the past, only what is yours now—your body, the people in your life, your dwelling, your occupation, your bank account. Though you have no memories of all the hardships that brought you to this point, you are fully aware of who you are in Christ.

You take inventory and plot a course of action in this life, having just arrived.

This is an exercise in storytelling that might help you see your own situation more clearly. What would you let go of and what would you do differently from what you're doing now if you had just arrived, fully aware of your union with Christ? Write that story from a new perspective and see where it takes you.

ALIGNMENT

Seeing with the eyes of Christ, which is my true sight, I see all that is before me in the light. In doing so, I release all of the judgments I have made against my body, my health, my relationships, and any situations that block my sight. Above all, I release the judgment I have made against myself for not seeing with the eyes of Christ. I know who I am and where I came from; I know what I am now in body, as a glorified being united with Christ, experiencing life in this form; I know how I live to witness Christ in all I see. In this prayer of affirmation, I see that I am free.

13

MY OLD SELF IS DEAD

I have been crucified with Christ; and **it is no longer I who live** (so the old self is a lie), *but Christ lives in me* (true identity)*; and the life which I now live in the flesh* (in an earthen vessel) *I live by faith in the Son of God* (by the Son of God's faith) *who loved me and gave Himself up for me.* Galatians 2:20

For me to live ***is*** *Christ and to die is gain.* Philippians 1:21

For ***you have died and your life is hidden with Christ in God****.* Colossians 3:3

(I live) *that I may* **know Him and the power of His resurrection** (and so to know the great power of our resurrection with Christ) *and the fellowship of His sufferings, being conformed to His death* (by counting our earthen vessel as dead). Philippians 3:10

Freedom in this life is found only in the letting go of who we thought we were. That old identity has been reinforced by centuries of false teaching and historical imprinting, which have bound us to the laws of fear and control.

A thousand times every month, a hundred times each day, we are transformed as we renew our minds according to the truth of who our Father says we are rather than according to the misperceptions of the old mind in blindness.

What the old mind was taught was in darkness was made of lies.

Here is the truth: The self that we thought to be us is not even alive. It's a facade, a mask, a costume, a temporal role, like a role in a movie. Our true life is Christ, because to live *is* Christ; and to die is gain, because then we will finally know how true this has always been.

Here is the truth: The life we experience now in the earthen vessel is going, going, gone. The lives we've led are actually "dead" and our true life is hidden with Christ in God. What is formed of dust and returns to dust isn't really even alive but for a moment in time, so we do not fix our eyes on it.

Here is the truth: Our journey now is to awaken to the power of Christ's resurrection and the power of our resurrection in Him. We do so by first conforming to His death in counting our earthen vessel as though dead. And, as though dead, we release our attachments to all of polarity. And as we release those attachments, we awaken to our true selves, already in Christ.

This is our resurrection.

What, then, is this resurrected life?

It's an experience we, as spiritual beings, have in temporary bodies, aligned to our identities in Christ—to our glorified selves in a love that holds no record of wrong and that transcends all law, all polarity, all smallness found in the empty philosophies and the religious traditions of man. In this we experience the kingdom of heaven here on Earth.

Thy kingdom come, thy will be done, on Earth as it is in heaven.

This is the good news! We are alive in Christ! All of our troubles have only been misperceptions caused by our blindness to our true identity, because Christ is all and in all.

PRACTICE

Write down any new insights in your journal. Note changes that you have seen in your attitude and experience in this life.

What is your body made of but a collection of atoms that have come from the scattered dust? It is filled with spirit, and spirit is who you are and always will be.

Unlike the Gnostics, we love our bodies as the temple of the Holy Spirit, but we do not worship them or harm others to save them. Today, imagine you lost your arm in an accident and had it replaced with a high-tech bio-mechanical arm. Are you still alive in Christ?

Now imagine the same happened for all the members of your body. Are you still alive in Christ? So, then, your earthen vessel is a fine creation, but it is not who you are. Journal about how this makes you feel and the freedom you find.

ALIGNMENT

Today, I release my attachment to my body, from the top of my head to the soles of my feet. I offer every part of me the love that holds no record of wrong, and in that blessing I allow my body to be what it is. Today, I release my attachment to my brain and all the cells that hold memory in my brain and the personality that my brain gives me. These are the traits of my earthen vessel and are not who I am. I am alive in Christ. For me to live is Christ and for my body to die is nothing but gain. In this, I find freedom from any fear of death, because I am alive and I always will be.

14

I EMBRACE THE MYSTERY

All that is in The Messiah is therefore The New Creation (the system of love); *the old order* (the system of fear and control) *has passed away to such.* (Perception of the world changes in that awareness.)
2 Corinthians 5:17, ABPE

*And they two shall be **one flesh*** (speaking of marriage). *This is **a great mystery**: but I speak concerning Christ and the church.* (Now Paul switches to our union with Christ, the great mystery, incomprehensible to Paul's intellect, thus *mysticism*.)
Ephesians 5:31–32, KJV

*And he who is joined to the Lord **is one spirit*** (with Him).
1 Corinthians 6:17, YLT

*I am crucified with Christ: nevertheless, I live; **yet not I, but Christ lives in me**.* Galatians 2:20, AKJV

We confess that we have been so indoctrinated and programmed by the world of polarity that conceiving of ourselves as Yeshua and Paul, and all those who speak of the great mystery, have described, is still often a great challenge to our old minds. So we return instead, over and over, to the law of separation and death and call it faith. Belief in separation is missing the mark, or sin.

But the great mystery is this: the two are one. We and Christ are united as one. We are hidden inside of each other as one.

There is no mystery to Christ being in us, like milk is in a bowl. The great mystery is our union with Christ, as one. Christ is all and in all.

How can two be one? In our common understanding, we cannot conceive of two things being one, thus we, along with Paul, are mystics, as are all who actually believe *in* the name (identity/nature) of Christ rather than just believing things *about* Christ.

We are one with Christ and we surrender to that great mystery, because only by awakening to our identity in Christ can we know that supernatural love that holds no record of wrong. The one who sees himself as separate from God cannot love as God loves. Only in union can we awaken to His love.

The church is the bride of Christ, an analogy that draws on human relationships. As such, the bride is His inheritance—meaning, all that He has reestablished in union with Him, foreknown before the foundations of the world. It's no institution—the bride is each and all of us.

But we aren't a bride that's *next* to Christ or *close* to Him. We are a bride that is in union with Christ, as one, and our fruit is the offspring called love.

Consider, as an analogy, one of the great mysteries of science.

Beyond the natural world we see with our eyes exists the subatomic field that makes up everything we see in material form. This is the quantum world of electrons and protons and many other identified particles. The study of quantum mechanics has given rise to countless technological breakthroughs in the last one hundred years.

Strangely, in the quantum world, none of these particles actually manifest as what they seem to be until they are observed, at which time they collapse into separate particles. Really, they are one energy. In what is called *superposition*, two particles seen as separate are actually one. They are strange energetic bundles of potential that are beyond space and time, and they defy our understanding of separation in space. It is mind-boggling but true.

If not for the discovery of quantum mechanics, none of us would have computers, televisions, or smartphones. No one knows how two atoms can be one— but we use the fact that they are to create amazing technologies.

In some way similar that is beyond our understanding, there is no separation between us and Christ. As written, each of us is *one Spirit* with Christ, who is the light.

And we choose to see all in that light because it is not our place to judge who is or who is not. Didn't Yeshua say to the vilest among all, the Pharisees, "The kingdom of heaven is within you"? If the kingdom was within such vipers, where is it not? This is not for us to judge, so we love all as the light, being the light to the light in all, and so lifting all in love to be reborn and see the kingdom of heaven within themselves.

All that is in Christ is a new creation. We now have life in union with Christ and so are hidden in God with Christ. We are not simply the bodies we see ourselves as, but *one spirit with Christ*, living in these earthen vessels for a brief time called this life, destined to have new, glorified bodies that aren't limited by time and space.

For now, our union and oneness with Christ are a great mystery, as Paul taught, and we surrender to that great mystery, which changes our perception of all we see and makes all things new.

PRACTICE

Write down any new insights in your journal. Note changes that you have seen in your attitude and experience in this life.

Using the quantum union of two electrons being one, as described above, consider the claims of Yeshua and Paul that we are one with

Christ. Could it be that awakening to our union in Christ is the basis for all that we might consider miraculous? Is it possible that the reason we don't see the miraculous like Paul did is because we don't see our union the way Paul did, and so can't fathom the power of Christ in us and in this world?

Write about the possibilities of truly believing in that identity.

ALIGNMENT

On this day I align my mind to the mind of Christ, because I know that God is revealed to little children and hidden from the minds of men. In aligning with Him in humility, I awaken to all that is possible in Christ. Without Him, nothing happens, and with Him all is possible, so, like a child, I embrace all that is possible beyond what my small mind has told me should and should not be. I am one with Christ, risen and glorified. I am in union with my Father and I am free.

15

THE TIGERS THAT STALK ME

Then he said to them all: "Whoever wants to be my disciple must deny (or disown) *themselves* (their blind, lower-nature self) *and* **take up their cross daily** (release attachment to their earthen vessel) *and follow me"* (into an experience of the kingdom). Luke 9:23, NIV

Do not store up for yourselves treasures on earth (world of polarity), *where moth and rust destroy, and where thieves break in and steal. But store up for yourselves treasures in heaven* (the kingdom within), *where neither moth nor rust destroys, and where thieves do not break in or steal; for where your treasure is, there your heart will be also* (you will be mastered by one or the other). Matthew 6:19–21

But I say unto you, **Love your enemies** (all that you think threatens you), *bless them that curse you, do good to them that hate you, and pray for them which despitefully use you and persecute you.*
Matthew 5:44, KJV

We say that the death of our bodies is only a passing of what is temporary. It is no different from losing a finger, or a brain, or a leg. These are all of the earthen vessel, which returns to dust.

And yet we have worshiped the body and our treasures in this life, fearing loss of what we value. As much, we have elevated the point of death as the great dividing point between eternal suffering or eternal damnation. And so, in fear, we have unwittingly become slaves to the death of our bodies.

But we don't need to live in fear any longer.

Today, we will remember that our glorified identity in Christ defines us, not the life or death, health or sickness, pleasure or pain that we experience in our earthen vessels.

Imagine a woman walking down the road beside a forest. Her mind is preoccupied with her husband, a cruel man who has deeply disappointed her, and her child, who has rebelled. Suddenly, a tiger rushes from the forest and she runs off the path to save her life.

But her way is cut short at a cliff, and the tiger is still coming. Desperate, she leaps off the cliff and grabs a vine, five feet down. The tiger comes to a stop above her, snarling. She can climb down the vine to the bottom of the cliff and escape the tiger, she reasons with some relief.

But to her horror, she sees that there is another tiger waiting at the bottom, watching her, growling. And to make matters worse, two mice—one black and one white—begin to furiously chew on the vine above her. It's only a matter of time before the vine will break and she will fall into the claws of the tiger below.

She is trapped.

In that desperate moment, with nowhere to go, she closes her eyes and surrenders her control. Filled with peace, she opens her eyes and sees strawberries on the cliff right in front of her.

So she plucks the berries and eats them and how sweet they are!

In our parable, the tigers represent all the threats we perceive in this world, including death itself. The mice are the passage of time in this life, day and night, with the end of our time here quickly approaching. The berries represent the fruit of the kingdom now at hand though fear blinds us to them. Only in taking our eyes off all the problems that chase us and surrendering to the light within can we see and experience that kingdom. And how sweet it is.

Ironically, it's those very troubles—those tigers that fill us with fear—that often lead us into a place where we have but two choices while we yet live: to continue living in fear, trying to control our lives, or to surrender our lives and see who we already are in the kingdom.

Only as we "deny" our small, fearful selves can we experience who we are as glorified beings in the kingdom beyond the matrix of this world.

To deny ourselves isn't a renunciation of self, which was the Gnostic way. Rather, taking up the cross and denying ourselves is letting go of our *attachment to* all that we think protects and defines us in our bodies, our relationships—indeed in our entire life.

Our journey is to let go of our offense so that we can experience the sweet fruit of love. It is to take our eyes off the tigers and the mice so that we can see the strawberries. It is to release our expectations in every relationship so that we can love without holding a record of wrong.

As we take the journey each day, we are filled with wonder and joy, because our journey leads to the end of all darkness—all anxiety, all grievance, all blame, all anger, all judgment, all victimhood—as we awaken to the light.

And walking in that light, we follow Yeshua's powerful teaching to love any enemy that threatens us and to bless the tigers that come against us.

Only then do we finally see that every tiger is our teacher, because those troubles, like the law, drive us to love and light rather than to the fear we see in blindness.

PRACTICE

Today, we practice the teaching of Yeshua by offering love to the tigers that have filled us with fear. But we can't do this with any force of our own will. We can only do so in surrender to the love of Christ that holds no record of wrong. In that light, there is no darkness, no offense, and no fear.

We surrender to love today by blessing what has persecuted us, be it our own minds, our friends, our bodies, or anything else that has come against us in any way. We will offer blessing to those tigers because we see that our resistance to them has only failed us and the whole world.

It is now time to try love.

Weeks have passed since you first began this journey. Many times you have released grievances. Today, create a short list of all the tigers in your life, no matter how large or small. Write a blessing for each, thereby offering what you saw as an enemy the light of the love that holds no record of wrong.

In so doing, you are experiencing the treasures of the kingdom rather than attaching to the treasures of the world bound in the knowledge of good and evil.

ALIGNMENT

Today, I lay all of my grievances on the altar at the foot of the cross to be free from them all. I surrender all that I hold against those who attacked me long ago, those who attacked me yesterday, and those who I think might attack me tomorrow. Today, I lay down all grievances I have held against myself for any reason at any time. And as I surrender my grievances, I awaken to a love that holds no record of those wrongs. In love's likeness, I awaken from blindness to sight, from darkness to light, from fear to love.

16

THE THIEF WILL NOT STEAL MY LOVE AND GRACE

And Jesus went into the temple of God, and cast out all them that sold and bought in the temple, and overthrew the tables of the money changers . . . And said unto them, "It is written, My house shall be called a house of prayer (alignment to God), *but **you have made it a den of thieves*** (requiring payment in exchange for benefit as opposed to grace)." *And the blind and the lame came to him in the temple; and he healed them. And when the chief priests and scribes saw the wonderful things that he did, and the children crying* (with joy) *in the temple and saying Hosanna to the Son of David, they were very displeased . . . And Jesus said unto them, Yea; have you never read, **Out of the mouth of babes and infants you have perfected praise**?* (This is the true response of alignment to God, who demands no payment for grace, unlike the system of sacrifice Yeshua overturned in that temple of religion.) Matthew 21:12–16, AKJV

***The thief comes not but to steal**, and to kill, and to destroy: I am come that they might have life, and that they might have **it more abundantly**.* John 10:10, KJB

*The One having saved us and having called us with a holy calling, **not according to our works, but according to His own purpose and grace*** (not our effort, but His grace), ***having been given us in Christ Jesus before time eternal**.* (This happened before time began.) 2 Timothy 1:9, BLB

Many read the story of Yeshua's cleansing the temple and imagine anger and violence, but we see here that He only set straight what had gone wrong with the whole notion of religion in that day. He was acting out what His own death and resurrection would do a few days later. The result was great joy, healing, and praise from the innocent. This is to be expected, because the good news of grace is celebrated by the infant in us all.

The religious leaders, on the other hand, were deeply offended by Yeshua's condemnation of a practice long held in their religion. All sacrifice is a system of exchange—payment for forgiveness—and those selling the animals for the sacrifice were only doing their job as they had for many years.

But our Father is one who heals, not for a price, but out of His grace, and this is praised from the mouths of infants. The mind steeped in blindness will recoil, because the old mind cannot fathom grace and love and so must justify its own demand for a price. Here, following His triumphal entry, just days before His death, Yeshua shows the truth: no price is required of anyone. It is finished.

As written, the thief is the accuser who comes to steal what is freely given us in Christ before time eternal. What was given us in grace is abundant life, which is eternal, beyond space and time, the kingdom of heaven available now while we are still in our earthen vessels.

The thief also represents judgment, which blinds us to the love of Yeshua.

Some will say, "But Yeshua told the disciples to take up the sword. Is that not His permission for us to do the same? There is a time for grace and a time for resistance!"

Yeshua did tell them to take a sword, just hours before His capture. And so Peter did. And when Peter then used that same sword to wound one of Yeshua's captors, Yeshua immediately healed the man and rebuked Peter.

With great wisdom, Yeshua had perfectly set up His final lesson before He was taken and crucified. His rebuke is clear even today: *No, that is not the way we do it in the kingdom—even in the worst of situations. Put the sword away, because to live by the sword is to die by that same sword.*

If Yeshua ever showed anger, it was simply His rejection of the system of judgment and law, fear and control.

And His great pronouncement echoes down through history still: *It is finished!*

Yeshua overturned the tables and cast out the moneychangers in a symbolic expression of the love He had come to show in the heart of us all. May the eyes of our hearts be enlightened to see that great love and grace in which we experience eternal life, now and forever.

May we join with those children and sing our song of joy.

It is finished!

PRACTICE

Write down any new insights in your journal. Note changes that you have seen in your attitude and experience in this life.

Many today justify their own judgment of others by pointing to the way Yeshua overturned the tables in the temple. In doing so we miss the point altogether and so the thief steals our grace. This was the point of His cleansing of the temple: religion seeks to turn grace into law. Two thousand years of history proves the same, but today we join Yeshua in overturning the tables in our hearts where we store the sacrifices we demand others pay for our grievances against them.

Think of all your own demands for justice, and overturn them one by one. Offer instead love and grace. Then you will sing the praise of the children who never were guilty, because grace was given before time eternal and love holds no record of wrong.

ALIGNMENT

I praise You, Father, for Your grace and love, given me before time eternal. I sing of Your wonder and proclaim Your love for all to hear. I praise You, Yeshua, for overturning the demands an angry world made on itself for grace. Nothing will steal Your grace from me, because I am in You and You are in me. The glory the Father gave You, You have given me, and in that glory, I sing Your praise. In this alignment of praise, I take back all that was stolen from me and I rejoice. You have given me life and life abundant, and I live in the grace of that life.

17

INNOCENT BY REASON OF INSANITY

But I say unto you, **Love your enemies***, bless them that curse you, do good to them that hate you and pray for them which despitefully use you and persecute you.* (Only in a love that holds no record of wrong is this possible. In such love is our salvation in this life and in no other way.) Matthew 5:44, KJV

Then said Jesus, "Father, forgive them; for they know not what they do." (Thus the Father judges no one as stated by Yeshua in the book of John 5:22.) Luke 23:34, KJV

When we look around, we see a thousand reasons to claim grievance against a host of wrongs, each of which, if we look at it long enough, might fill us with rage. And if we were to expose ourselves to all we've judged as unfair in this world—every starving child, every hate-filled speech, every deformed limb, every act of violence and oppression, every unkind word and selfish betrayal—we might very well scream with hatred.

Everywhere we look, we see the guilty and take offense. And in our own fear and anger, we are also guilty of joining the power of fear, thus multiplying it. Unwilling to accept our guilt, we project it on the world and take comfort. In this, the earthen vessel finds self-righteousness, coddled by the deceiver. But that self-righteousness is as filthy rags and so we find ourselves doubly damned.

What can we say, then, if Yeshua asks us not to judge? How can we love those whom we see as vile and cruel in such a dark world?

We only need to come back to our own guilt to understand how we can offer love instead of grievance. Isn't it true that everything we have ever done has come out of the minds we were born with and all of the programing that went into our minds through culture, fear, and conditioning? If we'd been raised in the bloody Crusades, we would have killed in the name of religion, as taught by all. We all act out of what our minds have justified on one level or another. As King Solomon's proverb reads, "Every man's way is right in his own eyes."

We get angry with those we see as wrong and justify that anger out of our imprinting. We fear for our children and loved ones, so we get upset with their choices. Most of us were taught that God is upset with us, so we are only doing what we think He does.

Consider Yeshua's story of the father and his two prodigal sons, one who tried to find himself through the pleasures of the world, and the other who tried to find himself through religion. We are all prodigals every day, but the real story here is the father's love.

When the first son asked for the father's blessing to go out into the world, did the father correct him or did the father offer his blessing, even knowing his son would find great trouble? The father not only blessed his son, but he also financed his journey. To ask for an inheritance early was a great insult, but the father didn't object. He actually *enabled* his son to enter the storms of life to find himself. What a staggering image of our Father.

But of course! Our Father has no fear and offers no condemnation. He loves all of His sons and daughters without fear of loss, counting us innocent in His eyes. We each get to choose how we spend our lives, either in the hells of pigpens or at the Father's table of peace and love, but we are always His sons and daughters, never condemned.

Is it possible for us to share the Father's heart for those in our lives? Can we offer blessing and love rather than fear and grievance?

In the end, we only judge that which we fear, and so, truly, fear has held us captive. Most of humanity acts out of its historical programming of fear and control, and that conditioning perpetuates our blindness to a grace and love in which there is no fear. Only forgiveness can liberate us from the fear and judgment that blind us to who we are.

Consider the soldiers who were crucifying Yeshua. They knew what they were doing, yes? They were brutally killing another Jew, as they had thousands before—each brutal strike of the whip, each nail, each thorn, intentionally placed to create suffering as an example to all. *Feel fear and submit to our control!*

And Yeshua's response? "Forgive even these, for they know not what they do." He was like a defense attorney making his case clear before God: "My client is innocent because she did not know what she was doing."

The verdict is plain: *innocent by reason of insanity.*

Forgiveness is letting go of offense. When we do not forgive, we must judge even more to justify our failure to forgive. And so the world is lost in the blindness made by judgments, which are like planks that cover our eyes to hide the light of love.

Only in letting go of offense against all, regardless of the offense, can we follow Yeshua. To the old mind, this is insane. To the mind of Christ, *unforgiveness* is insane.

Only in the forgiveness of Christ can we actually bless those who curse us, and do good to those who hate, despitefully use, and persecute the world. Only in this way can we hold no record of wrong.

The world is mad, don't you see? As are we when we judge. The whole world is insane in its blindness to true love.

And so we count them as innocent, and we, along with Yeshua, say to them and to ourselves, *I forgive you for you know not what you do.*

This is how we rest in the boat while the storms rage about us. This is how we love in a world filled with hatred.

This is how we surrender to the cross, where all offense was put to death.

PRACTICE

Write down any new insights in your journal. Note changes that you have seen in your attitude and experience in this life.

Imagine being in the Garden of Eden, before the fall, before taking on the knowledge of good and evil, which is judgment. Think of the Garden of Eden as the kingdom of heaven, now at hand and within. In that awareness, there is no shame for nakedness, which is self-blame, and no judgment.

In your journal, write down what your life would be like if you felt no shame, or blamed anyone for anything, ever. How would you be if you had no grievances? Take it further. What if you let go of all your preferences for anything to be different than it is?

As we consume of the fruit of the knowledge of good and evil, we join with judgment and fear, which is a form of insanity. Today, we forgive ourselves and the world for that madness, and, following the example of Yeshua, we count all as innocent by reason of insanity.

ALIGNMENT

Today, I place all of my blame and all of my shame on the altar of forgiveness as I align to the light of love in which there is no judgment. Today, I offer myself the grace of Christ for the insanity that has blinded me to that light for so long. Though the knowledge of good and evil has twisted my vision, I surrender that knowledge and awaken to the knowing of my Father, in whom I am hidden with Christ. And in this surrender, I can see a whole new world, free from the darkness of insanity. I was blind, but now I can see.

18

MY RESISTANCE IS FUTILE

*Ye have heard it has been said, eye for eye and tooth for tooth. But I say unto you, **not to resist evil** (some translations insert the word "man" here, but it is not in the Greek text); but whoever shall strike you on thy right cheek, turn to him also the other.* Matthew 5:38–39, DBT

If you love those who love you, what credit is that to you? *Even sinners love those who love them. (Loving one when they are being kind to you is hardly true love so has no benefit to you.) And if you do good to those who do good to you, what credit is that to you? Even sinners do that. And if you lend to those from whom you expect repayment, what credit is that to you? Even sinners lend to sinners, expecting to be repaid in full.* ***But love your enemies.*** Luke 6:32–35

Submit therefore to God and stand against (do not yield to) *Satan* (the great darkness that accuses us all), *and he will flee from you* (because darkness cannot coexist with light). James 4:7, ABPE

Science confirms that for every action or force there is an equal and opposite reaction. And in this plane of existence called the world, this is true in all respects. If we resist a hand pressing against ours, that other hand will only push harder. If one dominates a people with force, those people will eventually rise up in return. If a flower grows and blooms, it will also wilt and die. If we get angry at an injustice, our anger afflicts us in return.

This is the polarity we live in, bound by the knowledge of good and evil. What then can we do to transcend our never-ending cycles of pain and pleasure, comfort and anguish, ups and downs?

Yeshua tells us plainly, *When evil* (or the evil man, symbolic of all evil) *comes against you, do not resist.* In so doing, we only honor that evil as a threat against we who are glorified beings. And in honoring that evil, we give our authority to it. And in giving our authority to it, it gains power over us. And so we live in fear of evil.

This doesn't mean we allow someone to physically attack us—we best get out of the way, yes? But when we resist them with our hearts, we only join their darkness ourselves. When we say to ourselves, "I am angry at that terrible person for attacking me and I hate him!" we join their hatred and anger with our own.

We give evil the power it has over us through our fear and resistance of it. On the other hand, as we submit to God, who is love and in whom we are one, the darkness flees. This is how we resist the devil, through our submission to—our alignment with—God, in whom we are hidden and safe.

We don't try to sweep a shadow from a room, because this is futile. We simply turn on—align to—the light who is Christ. And in Christ, we are one with the light. As we awaken to that light, which is who we are, the shadow is no more.

In submitting to the truth of who we are, we turn the other cheek. We yield. We let the shadow of death be, without honoring it with our fear of it. We may remove ourselves from its path if it takes the form of abuse, but we don't attack it in fear. If we see another harming our brother or sister, we will stop them, but not in fear. Rather, in love, realize that the one harming only acts out of their own fear. They, too, are worthy of love.

This is what it means to offer a love that holds no record of wrong, which is supremely powerful, rather than offering fear.

What good does it do anyone to love those who love in return? Yeshua asks. None. This is not love at all, but the exchange of promises and kindness that characterizes most relationships. But when we love an enemy—this is priceless to us.

True love is holding no record of a person's wrongs *when* they are being an enemy. The only way to make darkness—that great devil among us—flee is to stand in the light.

This is our resistance: putting on the full armor of God, which is the full statement of our identity, one with Christ, as Paul taught. And this is the full armor of God: the belt of *truth*; the helmet of *salvation*; the gospel of *peace*; the breastplate of *righteousness*; the shield of *faith*; and the sword of the Spirit, which is the Word of God, *Christ* and Christ alone.

So we align to the *truth* of who we are in Christ. And in Christ, we see that we are the *righteousness* of God, *saved* from fear and surrendered to *peace,* and in this *faith* we stand.

PRACTICE

Write down any new insights in your journal. Note changes that you have seen in your attitude and experience in this life.

Today is the day of practicing nonresistance with those who always present themselves to be your most frequent enemy: those closest to you. This could be a friend, or a spouse, or someone in your family—son, daughter, mother, father. When you enter any verbal or ideological conflict with them, you defend your position, yes? Has it ever won you love, or has it only won you a passing victory? Truly, resistance has always proven futile, so why continue down this failed path?

What if, instead of defending yourself against their verbal attack, you stood in grace and allowed them their words of fear and anger?

What if, instead of resisting, you offered love? Try to follow Yeshua's powerful teaching, and then journal about your experience.

And when the accuser comes to mock your failure, allow that lie to be what it is: the darkness attempting to cover the light. In joining with its condemnation of you, you only empower it more.

Instead, offer yourself grace and love, and you will soon see your love shine.

ALIGNMENT

Today, I stand in the truth of who I am as the one saved from darkness. I am the righteousness of God, living by faith in the grace of my Father. I am peace in all conflict, and I join with Christ in offering love rather than resistance to what the whole world resists in futility. I forgive myself and all I see in darkness, and so I shine as the light that I am. I am the light of the world, and I stand in Christ.

19

AS I ALIGN, I AM BEING SAVED

Do not conform to the pattern of this world (the world of judgment) *but be transformed by the renewing of your mind. Then you will be able to discern what is the good, pleasing and perfect will of God.* (Only as the mind is renewed beyond the old patterns of the world can it discern the love of God, His perfect will.)
Romans 12:2, BSB

From that time Jesus began to preach and say, "**Repent** (*metanoia,* change your cognitive perception, go beyond your knowledge) *for the kingdom of heaven is at hand."* (Already here and in your very being.) Matthew 4:17

For the word of the cross (that we are dead to judgment and glorified) *is **foolishness** to those who are perishing* (those in blindness and that part of us that is perishable), *but to us who **are being saved** it is the power of God.* 1 Corinthians 1:18

The old mind bound in polarity considers the idea that we are one with Christ and so in union with God utter foolishness. How can two be one? How can Christ be all and also be in all? How can we have been foreknown and already established in the likeness of His Son before time began? How can the light have come into all darkness? All of this is written, and yet the darkness cannot perceive or comprehend that light.

The pattern of the world, as Paul wrote, denies any such truth. Those patterns are not the deeds we do as much as the beliefs we hold about the nature of reality. What we do always flows naturally out of what we truly believe.

Acts of love flow from the love that holds no record of wrong. Acts of fear flow from the denial of that love inside of us. So which are we aligned to?

Imagine once again that your brain is a computer and that you were born with an operating system that could only run Android programs. If you try to install an Apple app, it simply won't make any sense or run. Those programs are *foolishness* to your brain. Your mind can't even *recognize* or *see* those programs.

If you want to run Apple programs, you have to first reformat your brain and install a new operating system that can run Apple programs.

In the same way, the kingdom of heaven is foolishness to the old mind. We must first be renewed to the mind—the operating system—of Christ. Until we are renewed to that new mind, many of Yeshua's teachings make no sense to us.

"How can He teach that we are to 'hate' our children? It is madness not to resist the evil that comes against us. Why does He say that what we do to sinners, we do to Him? What does He mean, we are in Him and He is in us in the same way that He is in the Father?" And so it goes, teaching after teaching.

The only way to perceive the truth of our union with God is through a renewing of the mind, and Paul called this process transformation, awakening, sanctification, and enlightenment—all of which are the same process of being reborn into a new operating system called the kingdom of heaven, Yeshua's term for the same journey.

Repent, Yeshua taught, for the kingdom is at hand. It's in your very being. Indeed, it's within even the vipers, those Pharisees who serve the law.

The word for "repent" is *metanoia* in the Greek—*meta*, meaning "beyond" or "change," and *noia*, meaning your "mind" or "knowledge." Go beyond the patterns of logical thoughts that align to the world, and awaken to the light of your Father that is within you. Change your operating system and see a whole new world.

Only as we strip off the old thought patterns of the world can we experience who we are and find peace. This is how we are saved in the storms of this life. The good news of our union with Christ is foolishness to the old mind, which is perishable, but in truth it is the power of God for our salvation—the only way to find peace in the storm.

Today, we let go of all that we thought we knew in the patterns of this world and we surrender our minds to the truth of who we are beyond those patterns.

By this we enter into a repatterning, a rebirthing—a transformation that shows us light rather than darkness, love rather than judgment, and peace rather than the anxiousness that has held us captive through blindness.

PRACTICE

Write down any new insights in your journal. Note changes that you have seen in your attitude and experience in this life.

Think of the many patterns that you take for granted in this world. What goes up must come down. An eye is required for an eye, and every injustice must be punished in kind. If someone hurts you, you are within your rights to hurt them back. Some people are more important than other people. May the best team win. Property must be protected. If someone betrays, they deserve anger.

If you step out of a boat at sea, you will sink. And so it goes, on and on and on.

Don't conform to those patterns of the world, Paul wrote. So how does one break from those patterns?

There is only one way and that is to fix your eyes on Christ, who is the light in whom there is no darkness, the up without a down, the love that knows no fear, the grace that does not judge. All that was negative died on the cross.

It is said that pain is universal but suffering is optional. We accept pain as a function of our bodies. But that doesn't mean we must continue in fear and suffering.

In your journal, write a short description of who you are as the one who has the power to overcome all the patterns of the world. What kind of superhero would you be if you could express the full power of love rather than fear?

ALIGNMENT

Today, I declare my supremacy in Christ and I soar in that love that knows no fear. Though storm clouds gather, I rest in peace. Though troubled seas surround me, I walk in love. To the blind, the cross is foolishness, but to me, being dead to judgment is the power of God, which saves me. One in Christ, I am love. One in Christ, I am free. One in Christ, I am hidden in God and beyond all harm.

20

MY DAILY FEAST

I am the vine, you are the branches; **he who abides in Me and I in him, he bears much fruit** *(love),* ***for apart from Me you can do nothing****. (Christ is love and whatever is not done in Christ is nothing.) John 15:5*

Jesus replied: "A certain man was preparing a great banquet and invited many guests . . . **But they all alike began to make excuses** *. . . (the devout of His day, i.e., Christians). 'I have just bought a field . . . I have bought five yoke of oxen . . . I just got married so I can't come' (the blessings of God) . . . Then the owner of the house became angry (passionately insistent) and ordered his servant, 'Go out quickly into the streets and alleys of the town and bring in the poor, the crippled, the blind and the lame . . . my banquet (fellowship with God) will be full.'" Luke 14:16–24,* NIV

In many of Yeshua's story metaphors, He compared the kingdom of heaven—which is within all of us, even the most pharisaical, even the most destitute—to a great banquet. That great banquet is the fellowship of union in the Father and Son, a feast of eternal delights flowing with the fruit of the vine—love and joy.

It is to this banquet that we are invited each day, each hour, each moment of our lives. This is eternal life: to have fellowship with the Father, in whom we are one. This is our work while it is still day: to perceive the glory of God inside of us. We were born blind to see that light within us.

As Yeshua taught, apart from Him, everything is *nothing*. Literally.

Would any of us turn down the invitation to such a great awakening, then? Would we not all leave all of our attachments and rush to the Father's table?

Today, we confess—we acknowledge in simple humility—that we often forget the way to true sight that Yeshua showed us, and we live in sin, which is our blindness to the light of love. Like the people in His story, we are often distracted by the cares and concerns of the world and seek security where it can't be found.

What is most staggering about Yeshua's parable is that the excuses made by all of those who did not enter into the banquet were considered in His day as the blessings of God.

"I just got married and am on my honeymoon," one said. "I cannot come."

"God has blessed me with a new cow," said another. "I cannot come."

"I have fields that need attending so that my family can eat," said still another.

All of these were legitimate justifications, because they were all seen as God's provision in that time. But none of those blessings matter if we are not experiencing our union with our Father, which is the banquet of the kingdom of heaven.

Like so many of Yeshua's parables on the kingdom that is now here and within, some have interpreted this story as speaking about the next life, but that is to miss the point entirely. Truly, making the story about the next life only creates yet another excuse for not entering the kingdom that Yeshua explicitly taught was here and now and within even the Pharisees.

Our daily journey is to surrender our distractions and attachments to this life and abide in the vine that is Christ in us. There we feast on food that is eternal, and there we find peace, love and joy.

Apart from the love and light of Christ, we are actually doing nothing.

PRACTICE

Write down any new insights in your journal. Note changes that you have seen in your attitude and experience in this life.

Make a list of your great accomplishments in this life; they might be similar to the accomplishments of those in Yeshua's parable: a marriage, children, leadership at work or church, a party, a house, wealth, clothing, a legacy.

Now apply Yeshua's teaching to each of them and see where you have placed your value. If this practice disturbs you, don't worry. A thorn always offers pain while being pulled.

In Yeshua's teaching we will find great joy, because His banquet is filled with the delights of love and peace! We only must accept the invitation through our alignment.

ALIGNMENT

Today, I gladly enter the banquet of delight in aligning myself to Christ, in whom I am one. Here, as the glorified one, love is my food and peace is my drink, and in my joy I feast. I am alive in Christ and I bring that life to all I do in this world. When I dress, I find joy in my clothing as the bride of Christ. In all of my relationships, I offer love as the one in union with Christ, to Christ. In my home, I celebrate the beauty of even the darkest corner because now it is illuminated in the light of Christ. This is my banquet to enter and my feast to enjoy. And in this I am free.

21

I WELCOME THE COMING OF THE SON

For what will it profit a man if he gains the whole world (everything we think we are in this world) *and forfeits his soul* (the experience of his true identity)? *Or what will a man give in exchange for his soul? For the Son of Man is going to come in the glory of His Father with His angels and will repay every man according to His deeds.* (The great reckoning of truth versus falsehood that we all experience.) *Truly I say to you,* **there are some of those who are standing here will not taste death until they see the Son of Man coming in His kingdom.**
Matthew 16:26–28

Truly I tell you, **this generation will certainly not pass away until all these things have happened** (the coming of the Son in His glory and the terrible suffering of those who reject Him, as described in all of Matthew 24 and 25) . . . *Two men will be in the field; one will be taken and the other left. Two women will be grinding with a hand mill; one will be taken and the other left.* Matthew 24:34,40–41, NIV

At that time (the coming of the Son of Man in all His glory) *the kingdom of heaven will be like ten virgins who took their lamps and went out to meet the bridegroom. Five of them were foolish and five were wise. The foolish ones took their lamps but did not take any oil with them. The wise ones, however, took oil in jars . . .* (When the call for the banquet came) *the foolish ones said to the wise,* **"Give us some of your oil; our lamps are going out." "No," they replied . . . "buy**

some for yourselves." . . . *The virgins who were ready went in with him to the wedding banquet. And the door was shut.*
Matthew 25:1-13, NIV

Many have read the disturbing teaching of Yeshua in Matthew 16, 24, and 25, which describes the terrible suffering that will signal the coming of the Son of Man in all His glory, and they are filled with dread. But to we who are seeking the kingdom of heaven now in our innermost being, the news here can be seen as a beautiful invitation.

In Paul's writing to the Thessalonians, the coming of *the day of the Lord*, refers to a time when the *whole world* will experience the glory of Christ. But today we turn our thoughts to Yeshua's teaching on *the coming of the Son of Man in all His glory*, which is a different teaching, though often confused.

Yeshua made it clear that the events He was speaking of in Matthew 16, 24, and 25 would take place before His listeners' lives ended. Many say that the entire passage refers to the destruction of the Temple in AD 70, and this may be true, but no one saw Him coming in the clouds as He said would happen during their lifetimes. No one saw one man caught up while the other was left behind.

Still, this was how the disciples later interpreted His teachings. Indeed, as we know from numerous passages, even Paul was certain that Yeshua would physically return during his lifetime, and in this he was mistaken, as has every generation since Paul been mistaken. So we ask ourselves today, why did so many misinterpret Yeshua's prophecies?

For the sake of being drawn into an intimate awakening to our identity in Christ, what if we were to consider all of Yeshua's teaching in these passages as metaphorical for His coming into our full awareness? We can still allow for a physical fulfillment at some future time, but what if we were to apply His teachings to our seeking of the treasure of Christ in our lives today?

It was very common in the day of Yeshua for mystics to speak of spiritual matters in terms of physical images and metaphors. "The Son coming on the clouds in glory with His angels" was not an expression unique to Yeshua's teaching, but a typical mystical expression for great awakening in the heart.

And so we ask ourselves, how did all the things Yeshua prophesied two thousand years ago happen during the lives of those who were listening, as He said they would? How were two men in a field back then and one suddenly taken away? How were two women grinding at the mill and one disappeared? How did the Son of Man come in all His glory and separate the sheep from the goats?

If we interpret His teaching as a metaphor, the ones caught up are those who enter the kingdom of heaven through their transformation. In this way, the Son of Man, who is Christ, came into the awareness of some in that generation but not in others. Some are *caught up*—they come into a higher realization of their true identity and so experience the kingdom of heaven in this life. But others remain blind to their identity and so live in the experience of separation from God.

A man and wife might share the same house, but one is caught up in the wonder of transformation and the other is left standing still in the world of suffering. This not only happened in Yeshua's generation as He said it would, but also it happens in every generation. What might happen in the future as to prophecy, we don't know for certain. What we do know for certain is that Yeshua's teaching gives us meaning now, while we draw breath, in each hour.

In this light, all of Yeshua's teachings about the coming of the Son suddenly make perfect sense to us, and they fill us with an eagerness to awaken to the Son of Man in all His glory now, while we live. Interpreting His teaching in this way invites us to enter a new way of being during our lives—a way that is consistent with all of Yeshua's teachings.

When we take all such apocalyptic teachings to also be metaphors for the journey each of us takes during this life, we are deeply drawn to be the light in each day rather than to argue over what might or might not happen in the future.

The invitation to the banquet is offered to each of us every moment of our lives. We can enter that great feast and be caught up in the wonder of the Son with whom we are one, or we can languish in blindness.

And as the parable of the ten virgins makes clear, when our lamp goes out we are in darkness, blind to who we are. As that same parable also makes clear, no one can borrow their neighbor's transformation. Each of us is responsible for our own oil so that we might see in the darkness ourselves.

Today, we celebrate the coming of the Son into our awareness. Today, we celebrate our awakening to who we are as the sons and daughters of the Father. Today, we feast at the wedding feast, that table of great delights filled with the fruits of love, joy and peace.

PRACTICE

Write down any new insights in your journal. Note changes that you have seen in your attitude and experience in this life.

The practice today is simple: think of any apocalyptic teaching you know. It may well happen in the future as most have said. But now think of it as a parable that invites you to join in the awareness of who you are and so experience eternal life. There is no downside to doing this, and as you open yourself up to a new way of seeing those prophetic passages, you will find yourself rushing to your Father's table in union with Him. And so what a beautiful practice it is.

ALIGNMENT

Today, I pray that the eyes of my heart will be opened so that I might see the coming of the Son in all His glory in my life. In my union with Christ, I feast at the banquet of delight and I celebrate the coming of the Son in whom I am one. I am the bride and today my union with Christ is that celebration. Christ is all and in all, and I am a part of that all, and so I am one with Him already. And in this union, I have been made complete.

22

I OFFER CHRIST'S LOVE TO ALL

When the Son of Man comes in all his glory . . . *He will put the sheep on his right and the goats on his left. Then the King will say to those on his right* (the sheep) . . . *"take your inheritance, the kingdom prepared for you since the creation of the world* (that kingdom has always been here) . . ."
Then he will say to those on his left (the goats), *"Depart from me, you who are cursed into the eternal fire prepared for the devil and his angels. For I was hungry and you did not feed me . . . I was sick and in prison and you did not look after me* (you did not love me) . . ."
Then also they (the goats) *will answer, "Lord* (Christians call Him Lord today), *when did we see you hungry or thirsty or a stranger or needing clothes or sick or in prison, and did not help you?"*
He will reply, "Truly I tell you, whatever you did not do for one of the least of these (the sinners of His day) *you did not do for me."*
Matthew 25:31–45, NIV

Truly I tell you, **this generation will certainly not pass away until all these things have happened** (the coming of the Son in all His glory). Matthew 24:34, NIV

My sheep hear My voice (in alignment with me) *and I know them, and* **they follow Me***; and I give eternal life to them* (experienced now), *and they will never perish* (we are eternal and our suffering is temporal)*; and no one will snatch them out of My hand. My Father, who has given them to Me, is greater than all; and no one is able to* *snatch them out of the Father's hand* (an impossibility). ***I and the Father are one.*** (And we are one with Christ.) John 10:27–30

Once more we turn our thoughts to the events Yeshua said would happen during the lifetime of His listeners, and we quickly see that, metaphorically speaking, these same events are happening in our own lifetimes as well. And in them we find yet another invitation to eternal life, that state of being that fills us with joy called the kingdom of heaven.

Yeshua's teaching that many who call Him Lord (those who pray to Jesus as Lord and fully expect to enter heaven) are cast into eternal torment (suffering beyond space and time), because they don't love as Christ loves, causes great consternation among Christians. But perhaps we miss the point.

Here, He speaks of the sheep as those who love, and goats as those who do not love. In loving the least, we are loving Him, He teaches.

The goats in His story are only concerned with whether they are in or out of the kingdom and thus are surprised that they missed the whole point, namely, what we do to the least, we do to Christ.

When we are in the love of Christ, we experience abundant life, feasting at the table of the Father's fruits of love, joy and peace. When we are not in that love, we are alienated from the light, an eternal kind of suffering that isn't defined by time or space. This is the verdict of life in every moment, not in some future judgment. As we judge, we are judged, by our own actions, cast out.

Thus, we Christians as much as any, are most often the goats in Yeshua's story. But now we turn to Christ and see Christ in all because what we do to the least we do to Him, as He said.

The sheep are in alignment with His mind and with His kingdom and so hear His voice, like a song that sings of love.

Thus the sheep hold no record of wrong as they gaze upon those destitute and imprisoned in the shackles of life. The goats think sinners deserve their lot and so leave them in suffering, not realizing that without love, they turn their backs on Christ.

So we will love without holding a record of wrong. And in loving even the least in our eyes, we will experience eternal life today as the sheep who have ears to hear Christ.

PRACTICE

Write down any new insights in your journal. Note changes that you have seen in your attitude and experience in this life.

Our practice is to consider how each teaching of Yeshua's affects our lives today, and His teaching of the sheep and the goats is one of the greatest invitations to love one can encounter. Even if you think this passage must be interpreted as a prophetic teaching about some distant event, His invitation to love remains the same: "My sheep hear my voice, and in that call they see me in the least among you and so serve me."

There is no fear in this teaching, because we find ourselves as sheep or goats often, and so we find love or we suffer, all through our lives.

Today, choose to see that what you do to the least in your view, you do to Christ. In a love that holds no record of wrong, you cannot go wrong. Journal about who you see as the least in your point of view. Now bless each of them.

ALIGNMENT

Today, I see the least in my view in the highest light. Where I saw darkness, I see Christ within that shadow; where I saw ugliness, I see a beauty hidden from my blind eyes; where I offered condemnation, I offer a love that holds no record of wrong. In this offering of love, I am healed of all the judgments I have made against myself and my world. Wherever I go today, I will see with the eyes of Christ. Healed from my blindness, though I still feel pain in this body, I accept that pain as a part of my earthen vessel, and I am free of all suffering. In the light of Christ with whom I am one, I am free.

23

I CALL NO MAN ON EARTH FATHER

But do not be called Rabbi; for One (God the Holy Spirit) *is your Teacher, and you are all brothers.* **Do not call anyone on earth your father**; *for One is your Father, He* (God the Father) *who is in heaven* (the kingdom within you). *Do not be called leaders; for One is your Leader, that is,* **Christ** (spoken to the multitude). *But the greatest among you shall be your servant. Whoever exalts himself shall be humbled; and whoever humbles himself shall be exalted. But woe to you, scribes and Pharisees, hypocrites,* **because you shut off the kingdom of heaven** (the experience of divinity) **from people; for you do not enter in yourselves** (even though it's within even you), *nor do you allow those who are entering to go in.* (The spirit of religion seeks to control and mandate through fear and condemnation rather than invite with love.) Matthew 23:8–13

For the word of the cross (that we are dead to judgment and glorified) *is* ***foolishness*** *to those who are perishing* (and to that part of us that is perishable), *but to us who* ***are being saved*** (as we align with Christ) *it is the power of God.* 1 Corinthians 1:18

We have learned that we are hidden in God with Christ, one in and with Him. Still, the personality self is obsessed with its distinctions and personhood. The old mind thinks in terms of separation and cannot conceive of the great mystery of our true identity in union with Christ. Indeed, that identity is foolishness to the part of us that is perishable, even as the gospel is foolishness to all (including Christians) who are lost to their eternal self (perishing). And so we have difficulty entering into and experiencing our union with Christ.

Our journey is to enter a radical humility that allows us to release our grasp on the way we relate to ourselves, to God, and to others. In doing so, we enter or experience the kingdom of heaven now and invite all to experience it with us.

God isn't broken into pieces but is One. When we speak of God the Father, God the Son, and God the Holy Spirit, we may think of them as separate parts of God, but it may serve us better to think of the Trinity as three *expressions* of God that we, in our limited understanding, can relate to in different ways even though they are One, not divided. In our experience of space and time, we define God in particulars (i.e., modalism), leaning on the descriptions of Him that have been written, but He is One and surely transcends any description of Him in language.

He is also more intimate than we can conceive, closer than our breath, because the light is everywhere, as written, and so is Christ, who might be understood as the Word—that *expression* of God that can be known in form. We too are in Christ; so, then, we too are the expression of God, temporarily and beautifully manifested in form (bodies, polarity, human relationships)—all of what we call the world.

One of the best analogies we have in our world is atoms, which present themselves as both pure nonmaterial energy and material particles at the same time. How can this be? How can a rock be both nonmaterial energy and yet something solid at the same time? It seems impossible yet has been proven a thousand times over in the world of physics. In the same way, we are the essence or light of God, temporarily manifested as flesh for a brief time, and even as flesh we are purely energetic beings.

Imagine a seed that is planted in the ground. What does it consist of? Atoms, yes? The seed is planted and grows into a tree, made of the same atoms.

Now imagine we were to chop the tree down and take a branch from the tree to make a small wooden carving of a man. The wood is no longer a tree but a carving, and yet the same atoms exist, undisturbed.

Now we take the wooden figure and throw it in the fire. We watch it burn up. What has become of the wooden carving? It has turned into ash and smoke. But has anything happened to the atoms? No. They are still the same atoms that were once seed, then tree, then carving, now smoke, drifting to the sky.

If we were to take one of those atoms and split it, what would we get?

A sun. A release of more energy than we can imagine. Energy that existed from the foundation of the world and exists yet today, in some other form.

Whether in a seed, or in a tree, or in a carving, or in smoke, or even as a thing called an atom, the energy behind matter is never changed. It only expresses itself in various forms until it dies to one form and takes on another. In the end, it is only energy, and how great is that energy.

In a similar way, we, as the light of the world, are like that energy: not defined by the matter that we see as our bodies.

Science now knows that matter is only a temporary expression of energy, and yet John, Yeshua, and Paul all said the same thing two thousand years ago. How amazing!

In *The Way of Love*, we are beginning to relate to ourselves as eternal, glorified beings temporarily expressed as earthen vessels, but the old way of thinking still binds us up in the world's way of knowing, so we keep experiencing ourselves separate not only from God but also from our brothers and sisters. Our journey is to experience ourselves in the kingdom of heaven on Earth, and this means we get to let go of our primary identification with matter and see ourselves in the eternal realm now, a process Yeshua called being born once more, as an infant as it were, with a whole new operating system.

Surely this is why, as we have learned, Yeshua said we must "hate" or "release attachment to" all of our personal relationships on Earth, and in today's passage, He includes leaders and teachers among us. In other words, we get to release our clinging to all of our special relationships if we want to experience ourselves in union with Him, that is, enter the kingdom of heaven in the present.

Still, the small mind wants to break God up into pieces and break all of His children up into groups. It wants to break humanity up into special relationships such as mother, father, son, daughter, wife, husband, and on and on. As long as we do this, we will never fully realize our union with God and others in the kingdom of heaven now at hand.

In the mindset of a personality self, we can't help but think of our personal relationships and our personal possessions and our personal preferences as properties that define us. We are products of a "myself" culture and religion—*my* body, *my* money, *my* food, *my* house, *my* father, *my* church, *my* team, *my* car, and so on—and we pray that God will bless *my* this and *my* that. There's nothing wrong with doing this, but there is a much higher way of experiencing ourselves in this world, and that is in union with the Source of all that exists, and in union with our brothers, without personal possessiveness of any kind, as Yeshua taught.

We are all unique expressions of God in earthen vessels, but our tenacious clinging to what we think of as our "personhood" lends itself to obsession with self and separation from God and others.

Today, we take a turn to following the teaching of Yeshua by once more releasing our addictive clinging to all the special relationships we have established on Earth. And in doing so, we will follow Yeshua into the kingdom now at hand.

PRACTICE

Imagine that you had no preference for one human's well-being over another's, but rather loved all with a love that holds no record of wrong. This is the mind of Christ. Imagine that all possessions and all food and all well-being were equally shared by all who lived so that no one had more or less than anyone else. Then you would have nothing to defend, nothing to attack, and nothing to protect.

Does this not describe even our old view of heaven?

You say, that's socialism or communism, but both of those ideals were implemented out of the lower nature, which always seeks to control through fear, and so ran amok. But today we seek love for all in the mind of Christ.

Notice and journal about how your ego rises up in objection to such a state of being, wanting some form of specialness. Seek to reach beyond that small mind. See the love that would abide in a state of being in which you no longer needed to protect or defend anything, including a special identity.

The ego will tell you that letting go of specialness will leave you as *nothing*, but in reality, letting go of specialness will join you in the mind of Christ, who is *everything* and in whom you are one. True love can be found there alone.

ALIGNMENT

I stand in awe of my Father today. All that I have comes from Him, and all that I am is in Him. My eyes have shown me a world of things, and the world has told me that I am only one of those things, but today I see with new eyes that I am hidden in my Father in union with

Christ. I am His son. I am His daughter. And nothing can harm or destroy the truth of my being from before the foundations of this world. And so I release all of my attachments to the things of this world, and I soar in the love of my Father, free from the limitations that once held me captive. I am free. I am free. I am free.

24

ALL IS MADE NEW

The One having saved us and having called us with a holy calling, **not according to our works, but according to His own purpose and grace** *(not our effort but His grace),* **having been given us in Christ Jesus before time eternal.** *(This happened before time began.)*
2 Timothy 1:9, BLB

He **has made everything** *beautiful in its time* (already done but revealed in time). *He has also set* **eternity** *in the human heart* (the kingdom of heaven within us)*; yet* **no one can fathom** *what God has done from beginning to end.* Ecclesiastes 3:11, NIV

The creation waits in eager expectation for the revelation of **the sons of God** (all who were foreknown and glorified before creation, yet blinded by the knowledge of good and evil in the fall).
Romans 8:19, BSB

All that is in The Messiah (in Christ) *is therefore The New Creation; the old order has passed to such. And everything has become new from God—He who has reconciled us to Himself in The Messiah, and He has given us the Ministry of the reconciliation* (aligning ourselves and others with oneness in Christ). 2 Corinthians 5:17–18, ABPE

And the One sitting on the throne said, "Behold, **I make all things** (everything in existence) **new.***" And He says, "Write this, because these words are faithful and true." * Revelation 21:5, BLB

Do we finally understand now that the One who has saved and called us has done so for the purpose of Christ, in whom we are one, and not for the benefit of our earthen-vessels' needs to be gods of their own making? Only our blindness shows us something different, and so we seek to see.

Do we now understand that He has accomplished this in the grace of Christ before time eternal, not according to our own efforts in this life, as written? Only our judgment shows us darkness, and so we release our judgment.

Do we finally understand that He has already made everything beautiful in its time and set eternity in the hearts of all? Only false perception shows us something less, and so we surrender our sight to Christ.

Do we not finally see that we are the sons and daughters of the Father, in union with Christ, and so we, along with the whole world, eagerly await for the revelation of who we are? Only our misidentification outside of Christ, with whom we are one, keeps us aligned to our lower selves, but now we align to our higher selves, in union with Christ.

Do we not finally know that all that is in union with Christ is the New Creation already? All things have become new. Only our blindness in any given situation, at any moment, shows us distorted evidence that suggests anything different from the truth.

What are we to say then? Since God is for us, who or what can be against us? No one and nothing. We are free. We are free. We are free.

And today, in our last meditation together, we gladly surrender all that we thought we knew to know ourselves in union with our Father, because this is our ministry of reconciliation now. This is our journey of aligning to the truth of our being. This is our salvation in the storms of life. This is our sanctification in a holy awakening to the truth. This is our transformation of being born again into a whole new operating system free of judgment, blame and fear.

Only through that transformation can we discover true love: the love that holds no record of wrong; the love in which there is no fear; the love without which everything else, including calling ourselves "Christian," is nothing.

PRACTICE

Write down any new insights in your journal. Note changes that you have seen in your attitude and experience in this life.

Our practice today is to see that all things are new in the sight of Christ, and that includes how we see all that has been written in all of Scripture. Once you see what you have seen, you cannot unsee it. Your path will be one of aligning to what you have seen.

In the good news of our union with our Source, our Creator, our Origin, our Father, all is made new. Read any passage now and you will see a new story. The Old Testament shows us an old way of seeing God in a law that was weak and useless, as written. Its purpose in human history was to lead people to grace and love, which alone can save.

The Gospels show us a new story of that love and grace using ancient metaphors for the people of that day. Those few letters from the early apostles that have survived history further support the teachings of Yeshua in a unique way. Having seen the meaning of all that points to your Father and to the Christ in whom you are one, you are now seeing that truth everywhere.

As we come to the end of this book, write a summary of what you have learned and experienced on your journey through these meditations. Do you finally see what you were blind to before?

And so we rejoice together because Yeshua came to bring sight to the blind!

ALIGNMENT

Today, align through speaking aloud the following affirmations of what is written in the scriptures above.

Today, I know that God has made me holy for His pleasure and mine, in Christ, because I am made in His likeness. I know it was through His grace and not my effort, and I know that He did this before time eternal, so I am eternally grateful. Today, I know that my Father has already made everything beautiful in its time, and in so doing He has established eternity in the hearts of all I see. Now all of creation awaits in eager expectation for the revelation of the sons and daughters of God, which is who we are. As I surrender my old sight to the sight of Christ, I see that all things are made new in Him. My ministry is now to pronounce this reconciliation through a love that holds no record of wrong, even as He is the light that sees no darkness. And in this awareness, I see that light in myself to the glory and praise of Yeshua the Christ, in whom I am one.

So be it. Selah.
Amen.

THE JOURNEY FORWARD

Then the disciples came to Jesus and asked, "Why do You speak to the people in parables?" (Why so confusing?) *He replied, "The knowledge of the mysteries of the kingdom of heaven* (the kingdom is a mystery within, not the rational system the earthen vessel seeks) *has been given to you, but not to them* (those bound in religion, as were most in that day). *Whoever has will be given more, and he will have an abundance.* (Whoever has experienced this mystery will receive even more.) *Whoever does not have, even what he has will be taken away from him.* (Whoever has not experienced this mystery will languish in nothingness.) *This is why I speak to them in parables: 'Though seeing, they do not see; though hearing, they do not hear or understand.'* (I speak in parables because truth isn't understood by the earthly mind.) *In them the prophecy of Isaiah is fulfilled:*

'You will be ever hearing but never understanding; you will be ever seeing but never perceiving. For this people's heart has grown callous; they hardly hear with their ears, and they have closed their eyes. Otherwise they might (if not they would) *see with their eyes, hear with their ears, understand with their hearts, and turn, and I would heal them.'*

But blessed are your eyes because they see, and your ears because they hear." (The disciples, who were beginning to see, still misunderstood much at this stage.) Matthew 13:10–16, BSB

We finally come to the end of *The Way of Love*. We have applied ourselves to many days of meditation, humbly submitting ourselves and our understanding to the light of Christ. We could easily do another hundred on the many teachings of Yeshua that point to the same way, but we are already beginning to see.

And as Yeshua said, *Blessed are your eyes, because they see.*

In that seeing, you will read every scripture in a new light. Try it. You might not be able to explain what you read because the mystery of the kingdom is experienced more than explained. This is why Yeshua spoke in parables for those who had ears to hear the mystery.

And in awakening to that mystery, you, the mystic, will be astounded.

THE SUM OF IT ALL

How can we now doubt so many scriptures that claim we are glorified, divine beings, one with Christ who has reconciled the world to union with God? Yeshua taught that all are the light of the world but few see the truth of their being and so languish in judgment and darkness. We were all born blind with the specific purpose of seeing the truth of our identity in a world of polarity—up and down, good and evil, light and dark.

Yeshua called our transformation from blindness to sight, *entering the kingdom of heaven*. When we are blind, we see darkness. As we awaken to the kingdom of heaven, we see light where we once saw darkness.

The kingdom of heaven isn't a future or distant place we go to, but the dimension of light and love that is here and now, among and within all of us, even the Pharisees. It's seen through a perceptual shift that he likened to being born all over again with new eyes and a new mind. Unless someone is born again through this radical transformation that may span a lifetime or only a few years, they cannot see this kingdom, he taught. But the one practicing the truth comes into the light which is the kingdom. And that light is far greater than any human can fully comprehend.

Love is the evidence of being in that light. A love that holds no record of wrong and knows no fear, because in the light, there is no fear or darkness or judgment or grievance.

Judgment blocks our sight of the light as does all sin, which is a simple misalignment or a missing of the mark. Thus, most all humans live in sin most of the time. Judging others for their sin only further blinds us to our own.

Our journey now is beyond that darkness into the light known as love.

The truth is so simple that it defies minds born in judgment and self-righteousness. The world has returned to a punitive law attributed to God—a law that demands we each must believe and do the right things or suffer horrific torture. This is a system of fear and control that has further darkened our eyes to the light.

To see the light in which we are one with Christ, we get to become like little infants by humbling ourselves and surrendering all we have thought ourselves and others to be in blindness. In the end, the truth of who we are is good. Very good. And so we call it the good news, or the gospel.

Although we call ourselves Christians and have prayed the prayers that we were told moved us from one bucket into another bucket, we now see that we are often no more born again than any other. Our salvation isn't dry legal transaction that has left us powerless to love as Yeshua said we would. Our salvation is found in a life-empowering awaking to the light and love of Christ as we come into the truth of who we've always been. Only then can we find ourselves safe in the storms of life rather than cringing in fear.

And in this realization we find great hope because we finally see why we continue in darkness, blinded to the light. Now is the time for us to awaken to the light of Christ and so love ourselves and the world in and as that light.

As we seek, we will find. Remember that embodying what you are learning is a process that takes time. If you rush up the mountain, you might find yourself out of breath. Allow life to teach you as you persevere. Sight will continue to come even as it has already come.

If you struggle with any teaching, apply what you read to your own life—now, today—not to others or to a version of life that you might imagine beyond today. This alone will draw you to the love that holds no record of wrong, that is, the love of Christ.

Keep in mind again that *any interpretation of what is written that doesn't lead to a love that holds no record of wrong leads to something other than Christ.*

Don't be upset if other Christians don't see—they are on their own journey, perhaps bound in the old law and so being dealt with by that schoolmaster, which will eventually lead them to grace and love. Fretting over their journey is pointless; there is no fear in love. Our Father knows how to draw His children. They were born to see, so let them take their journey and show them love along the way.

Remember once more the parable of the ten virgins. Each was making her way to a great celebration with oil lamps, but five of the ten fell asleep and let their oil run dry. The other five could not share their oil with those who had fallen asleep. Why? Because we cannot borrow the oil of our neighbor's transformation. Each of us is responsible for our own journey.

Always keep in mind Yeshua's parable of the sower. Once a seed of truth comes to us, the old mind spawned by the father of lies can snatch it away so that the truth doesn't take root, and the joy we felt is stolen. And if that seed does take root, it can still be choked out by the cares and worries of this world.

We are each privileged with the invitation to walk in the light or stumble in the darkness—no one can make that decision for us. We are each accountable for the decisions we make, to love or to hold a record of wrong. We each reap what we sow, either more blindness or sight.

In the end, our Father, who is far greater than we can possibly imagine, will draw us to Him through His Spirit, even as we are drawn to Him now. In Him, we are far more loved and powerful than we can possibly imagine. The good news we will encounter as we continue on our journey is a bright sun that will chase away the dark clouds of our old mind, exposing the stunning truth.

The journey from blindness to sight and from fear to love is each of ours to take. Each breath we take is part of that journey. Like Yeshua's story of the prodigal, we are all prodigals who have left the Father's table, entered a world of trouble, found ourselves in a pigpen, and are now being drawn once more back to the intimate fellowship of union with God. This is our journey.

This is the journey of all.

Journey well.

WANT TO GO DEEPER?

THE JOURNEY CONTINUES AT
THEFORGOTTENWAY.COM

FROM DARKNESS TO LIGHT

A Contemplation on Suffering

For those who don't mind considering something quite abstract and aren't afraid to ask deep questions, consider one perspective on the problem of suffering that might shed some light on that conundrum. Feel free to draw your own conclusions, although allowing for mystery might serve us more.

Through science we know that true black is the absence of all color and all light. Thus, black isn't a color at all. In reality, it's no color at all and so does not exist.

In the same way, darkness does not exist but is the complete absence of light. As written, *darkness and light are the same in God's perspective* because He doesn't see the darkness.[1] God is the light in whom there is no darkness, as also written.[2] The light shines in all darkness. The problem is that the darkness does not perceive the light—it is blind to the light—as written.[3]

If God sees light where we see darkness, then it follows that our perception of darkness is a misperception. As such, darkness is *blindness* to light. The light is everywhere—we just don't see it due to our blindness to that light. And our blindness is experienced as fear, judgment, suffering, and grievance. *Seeing*, on the other hand, is experienced as light, love, peace, and forgiveness.

Darkness, then, is the absence of any experience of God, not because the light is not there but because we are blind to that light.

This is why Yeshua taught that if our perception is clear (true sight), we see light rather than darkness. And if our perception is not clear (blindness), we see darkness. In other words, both light and darkness are in the eye of the beholder, just as Yeshua taught.[4] Any particular situation can be viewed either with true sight, which sees the light (love, joy, peace), or with blindness, which sees darkness (fear, suffering, anger, guilt) in that same situation.

This is why Yeshua said that although we would have trouble in this world (perceive darkness), we can have courage because He has overcome. We will perceive darkness in this world, but in truth we have overcome with Him and are hidden in God with Christ, and in Him there is no darkness at all. So we can be glad and have great joy as we align to His sight.

In the same way that there is no darkness in light, there is no fear in love.[5] Fear is experienced in blindness to the love that holds no record of evil (darkness), as written.[6] Thus, fear is a lie, a misunderstanding, a deceiver that pedals illusions that don't exist in love.

Christ is the tree of life. Christ is the love that can hold no record of wrong. Christ is truth. Christ is grace. In Christ we see the light of love, truth and grace.

Darkness is the tree of the knowledge of good and evil. Darkness is grievance. Darkness is the absence of love. Darkness is judgment, sin and death. In darkness we are blinded to the light and we experience fear in all its forms.

In a nutshell, darkness is the experience of separation from the light, a misperception of the truth and, as such, not true—thus the source of evil is called *the father of lies*.

Again, in the same way that black is the absence of all color and so does not exist, darkness is the absence of light and does not exist—we only *experience* it in our blindness to the light. Though seeing (with our natural eyes), we do not *see*, as Yeshua said.[7] If we did see clearly, our earthly experience would be full of light without the perception of darkness, just like He taught.

Whenever we experience fear in any form, including anger, jealousy, anxiety, grievance, or blame, we are experiencing blindness to the light in whom there is no darkness.

But Yeshua came to bring sight to the blind.[8]

The journey from blindness to sight is the journey from fear to love. And the only way we can see in truth is to let go of our "seeing" in blindness, because what that false sight shows us is the dark world we have made in our own image.

May we humble ourselves and the ego's intellect, which insists on seeing darkness to maintain its grievance. May we learn to see the light of Christ in which there is no darkness and so give all who are suffering the permission to see light in the darkest of storms.

Only in Christ can we see that light.[9] Here, and only here, can we rejoice when we face trials. Here, and only here, our joy is full.

Here, and only here, the world is healed of all grievance.

1. Psalm 139:1,12, ESV *O Lord,* ***you have searched me and known me*** *. . . Even the darkness is not dark to you; the night is bright as the day,* ***for darkness is as light with you.***

2. 1 John 1:5, NASB *This is the message we have heard from Him and announce to you, that* ***God is Light, and in Him there is no darkness at all.***

3. John 1:1–5, NASB *In the beginning was the Word* (Christ) *and the Word was with God and the Word was God. He was in the beginning with God. All things came into being through Him and apart from Him nothing came into being that has come into being.* ***In Him was life and the life was the Light of men. The Light shines*** (present tense) ***in the darkness and the darkness did not comprehend*** (perceive) ***it.*** (And still doesn't.)

4. Matthew 6:22–23, NASB *The eye* (singular, perception) *is the lamp* (shows you or determines) *of the body* (our earthly experience)*; so then* ***if your eye is clear, your whole body will be full of light.*** (Proper perception sees light and beauty.) *But if your eye is bad, your whole body will be full of darkness.* (The state of most, most of the time.) *If then the light that is in you* (the light is already in us) *is darkness, how great is the darkness!*

5. 1 John 4:18, NASB *There is no fear in love; but perfect love casts out fear, because fear involves punishment, and the one who fears is not perfected in love.*

6. 1 Corinthians 13:5, WEB *(Love) is not provoked; (Love) takes no account of evil.*

7. Matthew 13:13, NASB *Therefore I speak to them in parables; because **while seeing they do not see**, and while hearing they do not hear, nor do they understand.*

8. Luke 4:18–19, NIV *The Spirit of the Lord is on me, because he has anointed me to proclaim good news to the poor. He has sent me to proclaim freedom for the prisoners **and recovery of sight for the blind**, to set the oppressed free, to proclaim the year of the Lord's favor.* (All states of being, not physical conditions.)

9. John 14:6, NASB *Jesus said to him, "I am the way, and the truth, and the life; **no one comes to the Father but through Me**."* (Yeshua speaking as the Christ, who is the only way to know the Father. Aligning with Christ, who's within us, is the journey from darkness to light, from blindness to sight, and from fear to love. We call this journey throughout life "being born again.")

THE FIVE SEALS OF TRUTH

THE TRUTH

ONE: God Is Infinite. He is the light in whom there is no darkness. Nothing can threaten or disturb Him. Nothing can be taken away from Him, making Him less than complete, nor added to Him who is already complete. God is good, far more loving and gentle and kind to His children than any earthly mother or father imaginable.

TWO: I Am the Light of the World. Christ is all and in all. I am created in my Father's likeness and glory. I am finite yet already complete, in union with Christ—I in Him and He in me. Nothing can separate me from His love.

THE WAY

THREE: Seeing the Light in Darkness Is My Journey. As I align to God, who is light, I align to who I already am as the light of the world—the son, the daughter of my Father, glorified and flowing with more beauty and power than I have imagined possible. In that light, I am complete.

FOUR: Surrender Is the Means to Seeing the Light. I will only see who I am and thus be who I am as I surrender my attachment to all other identities, which are like gods of a lesser power that block my vision of my true identity and keep me in darkness.

THE LIFE

FIVE: True Love Is the Evidence of Being in the Light. It is a love that holds no record of wrong and in which there is no fear. It is a love that flows with peace and joy on Earth as in heaven through the power of the Holy Spirit.

ENDNOTES

SECTION ONE

INTRODUCTION AND ESSENTIALS

1. Romans 13:10–11, BLB *Love is the fulfillment. . . It is already the hour for you to awaken from sleep; for now salvation is nearer than when we first believed.*

2. 1 John 4:18, NASB *There is no fear in love; but perfect love casts out fear, because fear involves punishment, and the one who fears is not perfected in love.*

3. 1 Corinthians 13:1–3, ESV *If I speak in the tongues of men and of angels, but have not love, I am a noisy gong or a clanging cymbal. And if I have prophetic powers, and* **understand all mysteries and all knowledge** (all the correct doctrine and beliefs about God and Jesus), *and if I have all faith, so as to remove mountains, but have not love* (agape), *I am nothing. If I give away all I have, and if I deliver up my body to be burned* (loyalty to creed and confession), *but have not love, I gain nothing.*

4. 1 Corinthians 13:5, WEB *(Agape) is not provoked; (Agape) takes no account of evil.* (Other translations: *keeps no record of wrong* or *holds no record of wrong*. Some translations insert "easily" before the word "provoked," but that word isn't in the Greek text.)

5. Luke 6:32–36, NASB ***If you love those who love you, what credit is that to you? For even sinners love those who love them.*** *If you do good to those who do good to you, what credit is that to you? For even sinners do the same. If you lend to those from whom you expect to receive, what credit is that to you? Even sinners lend to sinners in order to receive back the same amount. But love* (agape) *your enemies, and do good, and lend, expecting nothing in return; and your reward will be great, and you will be sons of the Most High; for He Himself is kind to ungrateful and evil men. Be merciful, just as your Father is merciful.*

6. Matthew 5:21–22, NIV *You have heard that it was said to the people long ago, "You shall not murder and anyone who murders will be subject to judgment." But I tell you that anyone who is angry with a brother or sister will be subject to judgment. Again, anyone who says to a brother or sister, "Raca," is answerable to the court. And anyone who says, "You fool!" will be in danger of the fire of hell.*

7. John 13:34–35, BSB *A new commandment I give you: Love (agape) one another. As I have loved you, so also must you love one another. By this all men will know that you are My disciples, if you love one another.*

8. 1 John 1:6–7, NASB *If we say that we have fellowship with Him and yet walk in the darkness, we lie and do not practice the truth; but if we walk in the Light as He Himself is in the Light, we have fellowship with one another, and the blood of Jesus His Son cleanses us from all sin.*

9. John 3:3, BLB *Except anyone be born from above* (some translations: born again)*, he is not able to **see** the kingdom of God.*

10. John 3:21, BLB *But the one practicing the truth comes to the Light.*

11. Luke 17:20, NASB *Now having been questioned by the Pharisees as to when the kingdom of God was coming, He answered them and said, "**The kingdom of God is not coming with signs** to be observed; nor will they say, 'Look, here it is!' or, 'There it is!'"*

12. Luke 17:21, KJV *For behold, **the kingdom of God is within you**.*

13. 1 John 2:10–11, NASB *The one who loves his brother abides in **the Light** and there is no cause for stumbling in him. But the one who hates his brother is in the darkness and walks in the darkness, and does not know where he is going **because the darkness has blinded his eyes**.*

14. John 1:1–3, NASB *In the beginning was the Word, and the Word was with God, and **the Word was God**. He was in the beginning with God. All things came into being through Him, and **apart from Him nothing came into being that has come into being**.*

15. John 1:14, NASB *And the Word became flesh, and dwelt among us, and we saw His glory, glory as of the only begotten from the Father, full of grace and truth.* **Hebrews 4:12,** NASB *For the word of God* (Christ) *is living and active and sharper than any two-edged sword, and piercing as far as the division of soul and spirit, of both joints and marrow, and able to judge the thoughts and intentions of the heart.*

16. Matthew 11:25, NASB *At that time Jesus said, "I praise You, Father, Lord of heaven and earth, that You have **hidden these things from the wise and intelligent and have revealed them to infants**."*

17. Matthew 11:30, NASB *For My yoke is easy and My burden is light.*

18. 1 John 2:27, NASB *As for you, the anointing which you received from Him abides in you, and you have no need for anyone to teach you; but as His anointing teaches you about all things, and is true and is not a lie, and just as it* (His anointing) *has taught you, you abide in Him.*

19. Philippians 3:10, NASB *That I may know Him and the power of His resurrection and the fellowship of His sufferings, being conformed to His death.*

20. Colossians 3:1, NIV *Since, then, you have been raised with Christ, set your hearts on things above, where Christ is, seated at the right hand of God.*

21. Ephesians 1:18–19, ABPE *And that the eyes of your hearts would be enlightened, that you will know what is the hope of his calling and what is the wealth of the glory of his inheritance in The Holy Ones, and what is the excellence of the greatness of his power in us, by those things which we believe, according to the action of the immensity of his power.*

22. John 17:3, NIV *Now this is eternal life: that they know you, the only true God, and Jesus Christ, whom you have sent.*

23. John 16:33, NIV *I have told you these things, so that in me* (in your union with me) *you may have peace. In this world you will have trouble. But take heart! I have overcome the world* (as have we with Him).

24. Ephesians 2:6, NLT *For he raised us from the dead along with Christ and seated us with him in the heavenly realms because we are united with Christ Jesus.*

25. Matthew 8:23–26, NASB *When He got into the boat, His disciples followed Him. And behold, there arose a great storm on the sea, so that the boat was being covered with the waves; but Jesus Himself was asleep. And they came to Him and woke Him, saying, "Save us, Lord; we are perishing!" He said to them, "Why are you afraid, you men of little faith?" Then He got up and rebuked the winds and the sea, and it became perfectly calm.*

26. Luke 4:18–19, NIV *The Spirit of the Lord is on me, because he has anointed me to proclaim good news to the poor. He has sent me to proclaim freedom for the prisoners and recovery of sight for the blind, to set the oppressed free, to proclaim the year of the Lord's favor.*

27. Colossians 3:1, NIV *Since, then, you have been raised with Christ, set your hearts on things above, where Christ is, seated at the right hand of God.*

28. Colossians 2:9–10, NASB *For in Him all the fullness of Deity dwells in bodily form, and in Him you have been made complete.*

29. Matthew 4:17, NASB *Repent* (*metanoia,* go beyond or change your thinking)*, for the kingdom of heaven is at hand.*

30. Matthew 18:3, NIV *Truly I tell you, unless you change and become like little children, you will never enter the kingdom of heaven.*

31. Matthew 7:9–11, NIV *Which of you, if your son asks for bread, will give him a stone? Or if he asks for a fish, will give him a snake? . . . How much more will your Father in heaven give good gifts to those who ask him!*

32. 1 John 4:18, NASB *There is no fear in love; but perfect love casts out fear, because fear involves punishment, and the one who fears is not perfected in love.* **1 John 4:8,** NASB *The one who does not love does not know God, for God is love.*

33. Luke 6:35–36, NASB *But love your enemies, and do good, and lend, expecting nothing in return; and your reward will be great, and you will be sons of the Most High; for He Himself is kind to ungrateful and evil men. Be merciful, just as your Father is merciful.*

34. Luke 22:42, NASB *Father, if You are willing, remove this cup from Me; yet not My will, but Yours be done.*

35. John 15:5, NASB *I am the vine, you are the branches; he who abides* (remains aligned) *in Me and I in him, he bears much fruit, for apart from Me you can do nothing.*

36. 2 Corinthians 4:18, NIV *So we fix our eyes not on what is seen, but on what is unseen, since what is seen is temporary, but what is unseen is eternal.*

37. Romans 12:2, NIV *Do not conform to the pattern of this world, but be transformed by the renewing of your mind.*

38. John 3:3, NASB *Jesus answered and said to him, "Truly, truly, I say to you, unless one is born again he cannot **see** the kingdom of God."* **John 3:21,** BLB *But the one practicing the truth comes to the Light.*

39. 2 Peter 1:4, NIV *Through these he has given us his very great and precious promises, so that through them you may participate in the divine nature, having escaped the corruption in the world caused by evil desires.*

40. Ephesians 4:23–24, NASB *Be renewed in the spirit of your mind, and put on the new self, which in the likeness of God has been created in true righteousness and holiness of the truth.*

41. Luke 14:26, NASB *If anyone comes to Me, and does not hate his own father and mother and wife and children and brothers and sisters, yes, and even his own* *life, he cannot be My disciple.* **Luke 9:23,** NIV *Then he said to them all: "Whoever wants to be my disciple must deny themselves and take up their cross daily and follow me."*

42. Matthew 25:1–10, NIV *At that time the kingdom of heaven will be like ten virgins who took their lamps and went out to meet the bridegroom. Five of them were foolish and five were wise. The foolish ones took their lamps but did not take any oil with them. The wise ones, however, took oil in jars . . . the foolish ones said to the wise, "Give us some of your oil; our lamps are going out." "No," they replied . . . "buy some for yourselves." . . . The virgins who were ready went in with him to the wedding banquet. And the door was shut.*

43. Matthew 13:7, NIV *Other seed fell among thorns, which grew up and choked the plants.* (Parable of the Seed.)

44. Song of Solomon 8:6, ISV *Set* **me like a seal over your heart, like a seal on your arm**. *For love is as strong as death, passion as intense as Sheol. The flames of love are flames of fire, a blaze that comes from the LORD.*

SECTION TWO

THE STORY OF REALITY IN THIRTY SIX WORDS

1. John 13:35, NIV *By this everyone will know that you are my disciples, if you **love** one another.* (*Agape* love, not brotherly love, romantic love, or friendship.)

2. Galatians 3:28, NASB *There is neither Jew nor Greek, there is neither slave nor free man, there is **neither male nor female**; for you are all one in Christ Jesus.* **Isaiah 66:13,** NIV *As a **mother comforts her child**, so will I* (God) *comfort you; and you will be comforted over Jerusalem.*

3. 1 John 4:18, NASB *There is **no fear in love**; but perfect love casts out fear, because fear involves punishment, and the one who fears is not perfected in love.* **1 John 4:8,** NASB *The one who does not love* (*agape* love) *does not know God, **for God is love**.*

4. 1 John 1:5, NASB *This is the message we have heard from Him and announce to you, **that God is Light, and in Him there is no darkness at all**.*

5. Genesis 2:7, NASB *Then the LORD God formed man of dust from the ground, and breathed into his nostrils **the breath of life**; and man became a living being.*
Genesis 1:26, NIV *Then God said, "Let us make mankind in our image, **in our likeness**."* **Matthew 5:14,** NASB *You are the **light of the world*** (speaking to the multitude).

6. Romans 8:29, ABPE *And those whom he **foreknew** he also **fashioned in the likeness of the image of his Son**.* **2 Timothy 1:9,** BLB *The One having saved us and having called us with a holy calling, not according to our works, but according to His own purpose and grace, **having been given** us in Christ Jesus **before time** eternal.*

7. Romans 8:30, ABPE *And those whom he pre-fashioned, he called, and those whom he called, he made righteous, and those he made righteous, **he glorified**.* **John 17:22,** NASB *The **glory which You have given Me I have given to them**, that they may be one, just as* (in the same way) ***We are one; I in them and You in Me**.*

8. Hebrews 10:10, NIV *And by that will **we have been made holy** through the sacrifice of Christ once and for all.*

9. Colossians 3:11, NASB *But **Christ is all and in all**.* **John 14:20,** NASB *In that day you will know that **I am in My Father, and you in Me, and I in you**.* **Colossians 3:3,** NASB *For you have died and **your life is hidden with Christ in God**.*

10. Colossians 3:11, NIV *Here* (in the knowledge of God) *there is no Gentile or Jew, circumcised or uncircumcised, barbarian, Scythian, slave or free, but **Christ is all, and in all**.*

11. 2 Corinthians 5:21, NIV *God made him who had no sin to be sin for us, so that **we might become the righteousness of God**.*

12. Romans 6:5, NASB *For if we have become **united with Him** in the likeness of His death, certainly we shall also be in the likeness of His resurrection.* **Colossians 2:10,** BSB *And you have been made complete **in Christ**, who is the head over every ruler and authority.* (The highest authority states our true identity: perfected in union with Him.) **Ephesians 2:4–6,** NASB *But God, being rich in mercy, because of His great love with which He loved us, even when we were dead in our transgressions, made us alive together with Christ . . . **and raised us up with Him, and seated us with Him in the heavenly places in Christ Jesus**.*

13. Colossians 2:8–10, NASB *See to it that no one takes you captive through philosophy and empty deception, according to the tradition of men, according to the elementary principles of the world rather than according to Christ. For in Him* (in union with Him) *all the fullness of Deity dwells in bodily form* (one with Christ, we dwell in earthen vessels), *and in Him* (in union with Him) *you have been made complete.*

14. Philippians 2:5–7, BLB *Let this mind be in you which was also in Christ Jesus: Who, existing in the form of God, did not consider to be equal with God something to be grasped, but emptied Himself, having taken the form of a servant, having been made in the likeness of men.*

15. Hebrews 5:7–9, NIV *During the days of Jesus' life on earth, he offered up prayers and petitions with fervent cries and tears to the one who could save him from death* (garden of Gethsemane) *and he was heard because of his reverent submission* (comforted by angels, as written). ***Son though he was, he learned obedience*** (came into alignment) *from what he suffered, and once made perfect* (having surrendered the will of his earthen vessel in that garden) *he became the source of eternal salvation for all who obey him.*

16. 2 Corinthians 5:16, NASB *Therefore from now on we recognize no one according to the flesh* (literally: the body); *even though we have known Christ according to the flesh* (when Yeshua was alive), *yet now we know Him in this way no longer.* **1 Corinthians 6:17,** YLT *And he who is joined to the Lord **is one spirit*** (with Him).

17. Romans 5:18, NASB *So then as through one transgression there resulted condemnation to all men, even so through one act of righteousness there resulted justification of life to all men.* **1 Corinthians 15:45,** NIV *So it is written: "The first man Adam became a living being"; the last Adam, a life-giving spirit.*

18. John 17:26, NASB *I have made Your name known to them, and will make it known, so that the love with which You loved Me may be in them, and I in them.*

19. Ephesians 3:17–19, BSB *And I pray that you, being rooted and grounded in love, may have power, together with all the saints, to comprehend the length and width and height and depth of His love, and **to know the love of Christ that surpasses knowledge**, that you may be filled with all the fullness of God.*

20. John 3:3, NASB *Jesus answered and said to him, "Truly, truly, I say to you, unless one is born again he cannot **see** the kingdom of God."* **Matthew 6:22–23,** NASB *The eye* (singular, perception) *is the lamp* (shows you or determines) *of the body* (our earthly experience); *so then **if your eye is clear, your whole body will be full of light**.* (Proper perception sees light and beauty.) *But if your eye is bad, your whole body will be full of darkness.* (The state of most, most of the time.) *If then the light that is in you* (the light is already in us) *is darkness, how great is the darkness!*

21. Luke 17:20–21, NASB *Now having been questioned by the Pharisees as to when the kingdom of God was coming, He answered them and said, "**The kingdom of God is not coming with signs** to be observed; nor will they say, 'Look, here it is!' or, 'There it is!'"* KJV *For behold, **the kingdom of heaven is within you**.* (Literally, *inside* of your very being.)

22. John 16:33, NIV *I have told you these things, so that in me* (in your union with me) *you may have peace. In this world you will have trouble. But take heart! I have overcome the world* (as have we with Him).

23. Colossians 3:3, NASB *For you have died and **your life is hidden with Christ in God**.*

24. John 17:3, ISV *And **this is eternal life**: to know you, the only true God, and the one whom you sent—Jesus the Messiah.* **John 10:10,** NASB *I* (Yeshua) *came* *that they may have **life, and have it abundantly**.* (Life abundant is the kingdom of heaven in this life.)

25. Matthew 5:44, AKJV *But I say unto you, Love your enemies, bless them that curse you, do good to them that hate you, and pray for them which spitefully use you, and persecute you.*

26. 1 Corinthians 13:5, WEB *(Love) is not provoked; (Love) takes no account of evil.*

27. 1 John 4:18, NASB *There is no fear in love; but perfect love casts out fear, because fear involves punishment, and the one who fears is not perfected in love.*

28. 1 John 1:5, NASB *This is the message we have heard from Him and announce to you, that God is Light, and in Him there is no darkness at all.*

29. Romans 13:10, NASB *Therefore **love is the fulfillment** of the law.*

30. Luke 5:37–38, NIV *No one pours new wine into **old wineskins*** (old identity). *Otherwise, the new wine will burst the skins; the wine will run out and the wineskins will be ruined. No, **new wine must be poured into new wineskins*** (new identity).

31. Colossians 3:1, NIV *Since, then, you have been raised with Christ, set your hearts on things above, where Christ is, seated at the right hand of God.* **Romans 8:30,** ABPE *And those whom he pre-fashioned, he called, and those whom he called, he made righteous, and those he made righteous, **he glorified**.* **John 17:22,** NASB *The **glory** which You have given Me **I have given to them**, that they may be one, just as* (in the same way) *We are one; I in them and You in Me.*

32. 1 John 4:18, NASB *There is no fear in love; but perfect love casts out fear, because fear involves punishment, and the one who fears is not perfected in love.*

33. Matthew 6:22–23, NASB *The eye* (singular, perception) *is the lamp* (shows you or reveals) *of the body* (our earthly experience)*; so then **if your eye is clear, your whole body will be full of light**.* (Proper perception sees light and beauty.) *But if your eye is bad, your whole body will be full of darkness. If then the light that is in you* (the light is already in us) *is darkness, how great is the darkness!*

34. John 3:3, NASB *Jesus answered and said to him, "Truly, truly, I say to you, unless one is born again he cannot **see** the kingdom of God."*

35. Romans 13:11, BLB *It is already the hour for you to **awaken** out of sleep; for now salvation is nearer to us than when we first believed.*

36. 2 Corinthians 4:6–7, NASB *For God, who said, "Light shall shine out of darkness," is the One who **has shone in our hearts to give the Light** of the knowledge of the glory of God in the face of Christ.* (In knowing God's glory, we see that we are one with Christ, who is our face.) *But we have this treasure* (our union with Christ) **in earthen vessels**, *so that the surpassing greatness of the power will be of God, and not from ourselves* (not from the personality, earthen-vessel self).

37. Luke 14:26, NASB *If anyone comes to Me* (responds to the good news of who they are) *and does not hate* (release attachment to) *his own father and mother and wife and children and brothers and sisters, yes, and even his own life* (all the masks we cling to in relationship to others and ourselves), *he cannot be My disciple* (cannot follow Yeshua into an experience of the kingdom now present within all).

38. Romans 8:30, ABPE *And those whom he pre-fashioned, he called, and those whom he called, he made righteous, and those he made righteous,* **he glorified**.

39. 2 Corinthians 4:7, NASB *But we have this treasure* (our union with Christ) **in earthen vessels**, *so that the surpassing greatness of the power will be of God, and not from ourselves . . .* **2 Corinthians 4:18,** NIV *So we fix our eyes* (our intention and perception) **not on what is seen** (earthen-vessel self and the world of polarity), **but on what is unseen, since what is seen is temporary** (changes in form) **but what is unseen is eternal** (the true spiritual self is eternal, beyond time and space). **Ephesians 1:18–19,** NIV *I pray that the eyes of your heart* (cognitive perception) *may be* **enlightened** *in order that you may know the hope to which he has called you, the riches of his glorious inheritance* **in his holy people** *and his incomparably great power for us who believe.*

40. John 17:22, NASB *The* **glory** *which You have given Me* **I have given to them**, *that they may be one, just as* (in the same way) *We are one; I in them and You in Me.*

41. John 9:5, NASB *While I am in the world, I am the Light of the world.* **Matthew 5:14–15,** NASB *You are the light of the world.* (Speaking to the multitude.) *A city set on a hill cannot be hidden; nor does anyone light a lamp and put it* **under a basket**, *but on the lampstand, and it gives light to all.*

42. 1 John 3:1, AKJV *Behold, what manner of love the Father has bestowed on us, that we should be called the sons of God: therefore the world knows us not, because it knew him not.*

43. Colossians 1:12, NIV *And giving joyful thanks to the Father, who has qualified you to* **share in the inheritance of his holy people in the kingdom of light**. **2 Timothy 1:9,** BLB *The One having saved us and having called us with* *a holy calling, not according to our works, but according to His own purpose and grace, **having been given** us in Christ Jesus **before time** eternal.*

44. Matthew 18:12–14, NASB *What do you think? If any man has a hundred sheep, and one of them has gone astray, does he not leave the ninety-nine on the mountains and go and search for the one that is straying? If it turns out that he finds it, truly I say to you, he rejoices over it more than over the ninety-nine which have not gone astray. So it is not the will of your Father who is in heaven that one of these little ones perish.*

45. John 15:5, 8–9, NASB *I am the vine, you are the branches; **he who abides in Me and I in him, he bears much fruit** (love), for apart from Me you can do nothing* (all is vanity in the earthen vessel alone) *. . . My Father is glorified by this, that you bear much fruit, and so prove to be My disciples. Just as the Father has loved Me, I have also loved you; **abide in My love**.* (Love is the greatest of all fruit, the evidence of Christ.)

46. Romans 13:11, BLB *It is already the hour for you to **awaken** out of sleep; for now **salvation is nearer** to us than when we first believed.*

47. Romans 12:2, NIV *Do not conform to the pattern of this world, but be transformed by the renewing of your mind.*

48. Romans 13:11, BLB *It is already the hour for you to **awaken** out of sleep; for now salvation is nearer to us than when we first believed.*

49. Matthew 4:17, NASB *Repent (metanoia) for the kingdom of heaven is at hand.* **Luke 17:20–21,** NASB *Now having been questioned by the Pharisees as to when the kingdom of God was coming, He answered them and said, "The kingdom of God is not coming with signs to be observed; nor will they say, 'Look, here it is!' or, 'There it is!'"* KJV *For behold, the kingdom of heaven is within you.*

50. Luke 5:37–38, NIV *No one pours new wine into **old wineskins*** (old identity). *Otherwise, the new wine will burst the skins; the wine will run out and the wineskins will be ruined. No, **new wine must be poured into new wineskins*** (new identity).

51. Ephesians 4:23–24, NASB *Be renewed in the spirit of your mind, and put on the new self, which in the likeness of God has been created in true righteousness and holiness of the truth.*

52. Luke 14:26, NASB *If anyone comes to Me, and does not **hate** his own father and mother and wife and children and brothers and sisters, yes, and even his own life, he cannot be My disciple.* **Luke 9:23,** NIV *Then he said to them all: "Whoever wants to be my disciple must **deny** themselves and take up their cross* *daily and follow me."* **John 12:25,** NASB *He who loves* (has attachment to, worldly affection for) *his life loses it, and he who **hates his life in this world*** (releases all attachment to this life) *will keep it to life eternal* (enter eternal life, which is experiencing the kingdom of heaven now at hand and within).

53. John 3:3, NASB *Jesus answered and said to him, "Truly, truly, I say to you, unless one is born again he cannot see the kingdom of God."* (Experience that kingdom which is, as He said, within us right now.) **Luke 17:20–21,** NASB *Now having been questioned by the Pharisees as to when the kingdom of God was coming, He answered them and said, "The kingdom of God is not coming with signs to be observed; nor will they say, 'Look, here it is!' or, 'There it is!'"* KJV *For behold,* ***the kingdom of heaven is within you.*** (Literally, *inside* of your very being.)

54. Acts 1:8, NASB *But you will receive power when the Holy Spirit has come upon you; and you shall be My witnesses both in Jerusalem, and in all Judea and Samaria, and even to the remotest part of the earth.* (Only in that power, experiencing union with the Spirit, can one be a witness.)

55. Hebrews 7:18–19, NIV *The former regulation* (the law of Moses) *is set aside because it was **weak and useless** . . . and a better hope is introduced* (the law of grace), *by which we draw near to God* (know Him intimately). **1 Corinthians 15:56,** NASB *The sting of death is sin, and **the power of sin is the law**.*

56. Romans 5:20–21, NASB ***The Law came in so that the transgression would increase*** (the more you try to fulfill the demands of polarity/law, the more failure it brings); *but where sin increased,* ***grace abounded all the more***, *so that, as sin reigned in death, even so grace would reign through righteousness to eternal life through Jesus Christ our Lord* (who we are, right now).

57. Romans 13:10, NASB *Therefore **love is the fulfillment** of the law.*

58. Ephesians 2:4–6, NASB *But God, being rich in mercy, because of His great love with which He loved us, even when we were dead in our transgressions, made us alive together **with** Christ . . .* ***and raised us up with Him, and seated us with Him in the heavenly places*** *in Christ Jesus.* **Ephesians 2:8–9,** NASB *For by grace you have been saved through faith; and that* (faith) ***not of yourselves, it is the gift of God***, *not as a result of works, so **that no one may boast**.* (Not even the faith is of ourselves, but a gift from God. Nothing about our union with Christ is of our doing lest one boast that he has what another does not.)

59. John 20:23, NIV *If you forgive anyone's sins* (including yourself), *their sins are forgiven; If you do not forgive them, they are not forgiven.* (Mankind's great power.) **Luke 6:37,** NIV *Forgive, and you will be forgiven.* (In forgiving, we free ourselves.)

60. John 5:22, NASB ***The Father judges no one*** . . . *Do not think that I* (Yeshua) *will accuse you to the Father. There is one who accuses you: Moses* (the system of law) *in whom you have set your hope.*

61. Luke 6:36–37, NIV *Be merciful, just as* (in the same way) *your Father is merciful.* ***Do not judge, and you will not be judged****. Do not condemn, and you will not be condemned. Forgive, and you will be forgiven.*

62. Matthew 5:14, NASB ***You are the light of the world****.* (Speaking to the multitude of outcasts, Pharisees, sinners and disciples.)

63. Matthew 25:40. *The King will answer and say to them, "Truly I say to you, to the extent that you did it to one of these brothers of Mine, even the least of them* (referring to the sinners of His day in context), *you did it to Me."*

64. Romans 14:10–11, ISV *Why, then, do you criticize your brother? Or why do you despise your brother? For all of us will stand before the judgment seat of God. For it is written: As I live, says the Lord, every knee will bow to Me, and every tongue will give praise to God.*

65. John 15:5, NASB *I am the vine, you are the branches; he who abides in Me and I in him, he bears much fruit* (love), ***for apart from Me you can do nothing*** (all is vanity in the earthen vessel alone).

66. 1 Corinthians 15:56, NASB *The sting of death is sin, and* ***the power of sin is the law****.*

67. Romans 14:23, BSB *And* ***everything that is not from faith is sin****.*

68. 1 John 1:8, NASB *If we say that we have no sin, we are deceiving ourselves and the truth is not in us.*

69. 1 John 4:18, NASB *There is no fear in love; but perfect love casts out fear, because fear involves punishment, and the one who fears is not perfected in love.*

70. Isaiah 64:6, NIV *All of us have become like one who is unclean, and all our righteous acts are like filthy rags; we all shrivel up like a leaf, and like the wind our sins sweep us away.*

71. Matthew 5:21–22, BSB *You have heard that it was said to the ancients, "Do not murder, and anyone who murders will be subject to judgment." But I tell you that anyone who is angry with his brother will be subject to judgment.* **1 John 3:15,** NIV *Anyone who hates a brother or sister is a murderer, and you know that no murderer has eternal life residing in him* (is not aligned with the kingdom of heaven).

72. 2 Corinthians 4:7, NASB *But we have this treasure* (our union with Christ) ***in earthen vessels****, so that the surpassing greatness of the power will be of God, and not from ourselves* . . . **2 Corinthians 4:18,** NIV ***So we fix our eyes*** (our intention and perception) ***not on what is seen*** (earthen-vessel self and the world of polarity), ***but on what is unseen, since what is seen is temporary*** (changes in form) ***but what is unseen is eternal*** (the true spiritual self is eternal, beyond time and space).